Massive Collection

Easy

Massive Collection
Easy

William Rogers

iUniverse, Inc.
Bloomington

Massive Collection—Easy

iUniverse books may be ordered through booksellers or by contacting:

iUniverse
1663 Liberty Drive
Bloomington, IN 47403
www.iuniverse.com
1-800-Authors (1-800-288-4677)

Because of the dynamic nature of the Internet, any web addresses or links contained in this book may have changed since publication and may no longer be valid. The views expressed in this work are solely those of the author and do not necessarily reflect the views of the publisher, and the publisher hereby disclaims any responsibility for them.

Any people depicted in stock imagery provided by Thinkstock are models, and such images are being used for illustrative purposes only.
Certain stock imagery © Thinkstock.

ISBN: 978-1-4759-9400-1 (sc)
ISBN: 978-1-4759-9401-8 (ebk)

Printed in the United States of America

iUniverse rev. date: 05/31/2013

CORRELATIONS

Dear Consumer,

Congratulations! You have just purchased a one of a kind puzzle that is geared towards education while also having fun. I have worked diligently to create a style of puzzle that is different from the rest and that would stand out easily above all the others. <u>Correlations</u> is a puzzle that is educational and equipped to enhance the minds of others. This style of puzzle originated out of the thought of making math fun. I wanted to create a puzzle that would help people learn or re-learn the basic math concepts and create different levels in which people could try to conquer. <u>Correlations</u> is suitable for all ages of people whether young or old. This puzzle can be formatted for those who want to take it easy and for those who like a little challenge.

<u>Correlations</u> is like an enhanced mathematical word search. I have enjoyed bringing this new style of puzzle to the market, and I hope you enjoy doing this puzzle as much as I have enjoyed creating it. Nothing is too hard to do if you just set your mind to it. <u>Correlations</u> is going to challenge you when it comes to math and searching for the words within the puzzle. Congratulations once again, and I hope you have a blast on your <u>Correlations</u> journey!

William S. Rogers III

How to Solve Correlations

- The puzzles consist of a 7x7 grid
- Solve the math within the box and try to figure out what letters go where
- You do this by knowing where each letter falls in the alphabet (EX: A=1, K=11, P=16, T=20)
- EX: To find the letter D you would look for 2+2 or two other multiples that would equal 4=D.
- Once you figure this out you have to find the words within the puzzle
- EX: GREEK – the words are not all straight or diagonal. As long as the G is touching the R box, the R is touching the E box, the E is touching the E box, and the E is touching the K box then the word is found within the puzzle
- The letters within the puzzles are only used once (**NO ONE LETTER OR BOX CAN BE USED TWICE**)
- All the boxes within the puzzle are not to be filled
- (1) (2) (3) (4) – These are used to identify the words on the Answer Sheets

Take this 7 X 7-square example on this page

34-12	2X2	√361	30-18	19X1	2X10	56/8=G (4)
12+12	55-46	5+2	12/4	169/13	√324=R (4)	25/1
2X2	10+10	60-45=O (2)	3X3	30-15	3X5=O (4)	26-13
45/9	√529=W (2)	64/8=H (1)	3X4=L (2)	144/12=L (2)	36/6	46-23=W (4)
81-9	78-66	36-18=R (1)	12+8=T (1)	20+3	√225=O (2)	28-14=N (4)
4+1=E (3)	25-20=E (1)	22-8=N (3)	3X5=O (1)	2X11=V (3)	16/4=D (3)	36/6=F (2)
1X1	9-6=C (3)	√196=N (1)	1+0=A (3)	24/24=A (3)	12+5	5-3

WORDS

1. THRONE (20, 8, 18, 15, 14, 5)
2. FOLLOW (6, 15, 12, 12, 15, 23)
3. ADVANCE (1, 4, 22, 1, 14, 3, 5)
4. GROWN (7, 18, 15, 23, 14)

To start, look for a word that have letters that are not in the other words. The word GROWN; locate the letter G first by looking for all the multiples that comes out to equal 7=G. There are only 2 boxes that comes out to equal 7; 5+2 above the 60-45=O box and 56/8 box up in the right hand corner. The one in the upper right hand corner is the only one that has an R box connected to it. Once the R box is found with √324 there are two O boxes connected to it. There is one directly below this box and then there is one on the left that is diagonal from it. When this arises, you have to plan ahead and look for the next letter which would be the letter W. The only logical move to make after planning ahead is to go with the O box that is directly under the R box. After this is found, the 46-23=W box which determined which O box would be used by planning ahead is than found. From there the N box is found with 28-14. The word GROWN is now found within the puzzle. All the letters have to connect in order for the word to be found within the puzzle. In cases like trying to find the word GROWN, plan ahead and locate the other letters within the word you are trying to find. After the word GROWN is found use the Elimination Process (finding a word and not being able to reuse those same boxes over again) if another problem arises like this one.

If one discovers that a word is too hard to find, locate part of the word within the puzzle first, stop, and search for a new word. This often helps because searching for a new word can eliminate some of the boxes that you may have thought were going to be used for the first word you were searching for. There is no guess work that needs to be done when it comes to these puzzles. All you have to do is solve the math, plan ahead, look at surrounding boxes, and figure out where the words are within the puzzle. Use these tips in order to continue finding the rest of the words within the puzzle.

Additional Tips

- **Try to solve the math within the box to find the words within the puzzle**
- **Try and look for letters that are not in other words**
- **In puzzles that have similar letters within words, try and find the letters that are the same (It sometimes help to look for a word backwards, starting with the last letter in the word)**
- **Remember, you can only use a box once; so try and plan ahead**

Square Roots

A =1	$\sqrt{1}$	N = 14	$\sqrt{196}$
B = 2	$\sqrt{4}$	O = 15	$\sqrt{225}$
C = 3	$\sqrt{9}$	P = 16	$\sqrt{256}$
D = 4	$\sqrt{16}$	Q = 17	$\sqrt{289}$
E = 5	$\sqrt{25}$	R = 18	$\sqrt{324}$
F = 6	$\sqrt{36}$	S = 19	$\sqrt{361}$
G = 7	$\sqrt{49}$	T = 20	$\sqrt{400}$
H = 8	$\sqrt{64}$	U = 21	$\sqrt{441}$
I = 9	$\sqrt{81}$	V = 22	$\sqrt{484}$
J = 10	$\sqrt{100}$	W = 23	$\sqrt{529}$
K = 11	$\sqrt{121}$	X = 24	$\sqrt{576}$
L = 12	$\sqrt{144}$	Y = 25	$\sqrt{625}$
M = 13	$\sqrt{169}$	Z = 26	$\sqrt{676}$

EASY

2X2	10+10	25/5	36/12	26-18	√441	√256
2+3	√361	4+5	12-1	36-18	45-34	2X2
12+10	34-12	400/20	1+0	8+8	30-11	9+1
72/8	25/5	64/8	26-13	36-19	64/8	2X6
63/9	1X1	4X4	3X3	19X1	13-12	√169
2+3	4+12	24-12	3X5	6+6	10+5	14+4
16/4	49/7	√144	1X1	45-42	5X5	20-12

WORDS

1. LOCALS
2. CRAMP
3. STEAL
4. MORALS

EASY

10+10	400/20	25-12	46-35	3X2	12+1	15+5
324/18	225/15	4+4	36-24	32/8	√400	18-9
32-16	25/5	25-24	3+2	2X9	3+1	72/8
16/4	3X1	√441	8/4	3+6	3X5	8X2
5X5	25-10	√169	56/8	38-19	21/7	3+1
12+13	3X5	2X4	√324	324/18	5X1	√144
√169	8X2	2+12	2X5	√81	10+10	1X1

WORDS

1. LAUGH
2. CRIED
3. COMBS
4. TRIED

EASY

2X10	28-14	10+10	45-32	2X3	9/3	4X1
15-12	15/3	√361	14+5	√324	√225	10+1
4X5	25/5	2+2	72/8	225/15	60/5	40/10
64/8	3X4	10+10	2X4	7+2	5X1	12+12
144/12	30-11	5X1	72/8	√49	36/6	30-16
4+5	26-16	36-18	4X5	√625	36-18	20-12
31-17	34-23	3X1	12-10	441/21	√225	√121

WORDS

1. LIGHTS
2. YIELD
3. BURNED
4. CROSS

EASY

2X2	12+12	25-21	225/15	49/7	3X1	21-16
10+10	3X3	18-9	22-12	1+3	15+6	24/12
25/5	49/7	81-78	19X1	15/3	18/9	35/7
2X2	3X1	5+12	3X5	4+3	3+2	√144
√121	√225	72/6	2X7	46-23	√400	10+8
√256	45/9	45/5	26/13	5X1	196/14	√196
2X3	16/4	√361	36-24	81/9	2+2	32-27

WORDS

1. BLOWER
2. SINGS
3. BELTED
4. LINEN

EASY

4X5	12+10	26/13	4X1	26-17	30-11	34-12
100/10	121/11	√225	√484	7-2	3X1	12+1
30-19	2X7	22-14	5X1	√484	1X1	1+1
10+9	3X1	7X1	1X1	3X3	100-88	24-12
49-47	34-11	18-9	12+8	25/5	144/12	36-18
2X1	19+1	11+8	9-4	1X1	√324	12/4
√324	√225	4+8	√529	√324	√256	7X1

WORDS

1. LEAVE
2. STILL
3. REIGN
4. CRAWL

EASY

2+2	15-4	36/6	4X2	√121	2X1	36-34
108/9	3X3	2X2	48/4	2X6	14-7	16-8
10+10	15+4	30-15	25-20	2X9	289/17	30-16
32-16	28-23	4+1	12+10	361/19	3X3	3+2
12+8	30-12	7X1	√225	√400	2X2	42/6
14-13	18-9	144/12	64/8	√81	49/7	12/12
17-14	27/9	10+9	60/5	90/5	2X2	3+3

WORDS

1. LOVER
2. DIGGING
3. SIGHT
4. CLOSED

EASY

3X4	14-7	2X9	19X1	36-18	45-40	√361
√361	225/15	12-6	3X4	1+2	√256	12+7
196/14	26-13	42/3	1X1	57/3	3X3	36-18
3X1	18-9	3X3	5X1	38-19	1X1	√484
10+10	√529	24-12	81/9	16/4	15-6	√529
43-23	3X4	√196	3X5	3+2	12+3	15-4
√169	√121	36-30	25/5	2X7	19X1	14-6

WORDS

1. VISION
2. FAILED
3. KNEES
4. WARPS

EASY

24-23	3+2	13+6	17-12	3X1	24/12	36/6
√121	324/18	30-10	2X11	46-23	√441	3X4
99/9	5+5	22-11	20-6	3X5	8+7	40-20
45/3	43-29	3X1	81/9	2X7	15+5	10+2
√484	46-23	√400	5+4	5X1	√225	50/2
√36	2X8	2X1	12+8	324/18	11+3	√64
72/8	2X2	14-6	3+2	7+8	√400	12/12

WORDS

1. KITTEN
2. BUTTON
3. FLOWN
4. TRIBE

EASY

18-9	3X5	24/6	12-10	15/15	30/5	√400
100/10	25/5	30-12	3+2	4X2	√324	2+1
√676	225/15	2X2	5+4	15-8	18-9	4+3
529/23	56/7	3+2	3X2	7X1	1+4	42/7
63/7	12+6	96/8	324/18	1X1	64/8	3X3
4+7	10+11	3X3	25/5	5X1	√400	121/11
√144	60/4	57/3	40-20	3+3	4+1	15/3

WORDS

1. WRITE
2. RIGHT
3. RIFLE
4. FEARED

EASY

√324	45/5	26-13	3+2	√169	14-3	16-8
3X3	√484	7+2	1X1	676/26	26-13	15+10
2X9	19X1	3+4	√81	60/5	76/4	√121
√196	14-6	38-19	225/15	4+8	19X1	144/12
2X7	25/5	23-3	10-5	√49	63/7	3+2
7+4	√361	10+10	4X4	16-12	12/12	√121
19X1	1+0	45-43	5X1	2X7	√36	42/6

WORDS

1. GOTTEN
2. MAILED
3. LIKES
4. MISSES

EASY

46-23	18+5	3X7	√625	25-10	6+7	1X1
225/15	√625	20-8	324/18	√400	36-18	6+6
144/12	12+8	2X3	64/8	4+5	15+4	5/1
19X1	3X4	361/19	√49	3X3	4X4	4+3
484/22	10+10	√225	28-14	2X7	30-15	2X8
15-14	3+6	56/8	√169	18-9	441/21	36/2
38-19	3X4	19X1	15+5	42/6	48-42	6/2

WORDS

1. THINGS
2. GOING
3. MOSTLY
4. UPPER

EASY

100/10	256/16	25/5	3+1	√441	44-22	2X1
12+12	3X5	50/10	2X7	√625	√529	23-13
40-20	3+2	35/7	36-18	2X10	15-4	3+2
3X4	8+8	2X2	25/5	18/9	19-18	3X3
15-4	19X1	32-16	24-12	11+4	30-14	30/5
35/7	6X2	225/15	√256	3X5	√9	√324
361/19	13+3	25-5	14-7	10+4	√361	16/16

WORDS

1. COPPER
2. GOLDEN
3. WEAPONS
4. PEEPS

EASY

2X10	14-5	144/12	3X3	38-19	19-8	15+4
10+10	√324	20/10	10-5	√484	√441	72/9
441/21	90/18	36-18	1X1	√256	1X1	√225
2X2	16/16	4+3	3+2	56/8	√169	16-8
225/15	42/3	√49	25/25	46-23	5X1	32-16
2X8	14-7	15/3	5X1	361/19	3X7	24/6
4+6	43-40	4+3	16/4	3+2	√529	484/22

WORDS

1. WEEDS
2. BAGGAGE
3. HAMPER
4. HOUSE

EASY

12/3	4X4	25/5	12+3	√324	38-19	24-7
√225	45/5	3X2	5X1	√49	12+1	15/15
64/8	√100	√169	20/4	√121	3+2	42/6
10+10	3X4	28-14	225/15	1X1	64/8	144/12
42/3	2X2	19X1	√484	26-13	45-30	57/3
76/4	28/2	36-18	3+2	18-9	12+7	38-19
2X9	3+5	6+6	144/12	√121	225/15	√400

WORDS

1. MOVIES
2. GHOST
3. LEGEND
4. MAKERS

EASY

15+5	3X2	14-5	√225	289/17	13+3	5-4
13/13	6X1	4+6	20-8	11-10	10+10	24/4
√169	196/14	25-20	2X10	4/2	√25	20-3
36/6	42/6	4+1	36/3	169/13	10+8	√361
13+3	4X3	√36	14+4	√441	√529	1+2
√144	√225	5X1	81/9	3X3	16-8	18-9
3X3	2X2	30-12	14/14	256/16	√441	21-3

WORDS

1. HUMBLE
2. FIRED
3. SWIRL
4. CREATE

EASY

400/20	2X1	14/14	√324	1+2	√225	38-19
10+6	225/15	3X1	3X3	30-15	5X1	4+1
13+6	17-5	3X6	√169	40-20	10+5	√256
324/18	16/4	1X1	361/19	√529	√225	3X4
√100	√225	2X7	4+4	√16	√196	144/12
4X3	30-10	9/3	3+2	12/3	20/4	16-3
8+7	25/5	4X5	√64	√625	90/5	26/13

WORDS

1. ROMANCE
2. NOTICE
3. YELLOW
4. DOTTED

EASY

3X4	15-4	12+4	√361	28-14	33-23	3X1
√169	196/14	√324	3X2	14-5	8X2	2X2
2+3	64/8	10+9	25/5	72/8	√25	3X3
4+4	3X3	19X1	32-16	√81	225/15	40-20
√441	2X4	1X1	4+3	72/9	1+0	54/9
3X7	1+2	√529	38-19	2X7	144/12	2+2
42/3	48/3	16-8	18-9	3X3	25/5	34-23

WORDS

1. CASHIER
2. FLINGS
3. DATED
4. WHISP

EASY

16-5	2X2	22/11	12+8	42/3	57-45	256/16
2X4	2+3	2X9	14/14	3X5	225/15	√289
324/18	10-4	3+6	2X9	30-11	24-12	6/2
100/5	24/4	3X3	32-16	19X1	15+5	2X2
10+5	2+2	√225	144/12	3X3	√81	72/9
4+4	6/2	2+3	√441	10-5	49/7	12+7
21/3	√225	√361	34/2	2X1	24-12	36-18

WORDS

1. TRIPLE
2. DIGITS
3. DOUBLE
4. COLORS

EASY

256/16	2X2	12+2	12+8	25-20	√441	24-12
33-23	27-4	3X3	20-11	√256	49/7	√289
√225	625/25	√400	25/5	2X7	√361	20-6
√676	32-21	45/9	5X1	21/3	1X1	3X3
25/5	15+4	36-18	10-5	40/20	64/8	45/45
19X1	10+10	6+7	2+1	5X1	4+3	34-14
√256	144/12	12/3	3+3	√324	4X2	15/5

WORDS

1. CREEPS
2. MEETING
3. GATHER
4. BANQUET

EASY

12+2	225/15	5X1	√144	4+5	6+6	26-13
5+6	10+8	46-23	√121	5X5	1X1	144/12
60/5	19X1	12-3	2X5	3X6	24-12	9-6
100/20	75/5	√324	3+2	30-9	√225	81/9
90/5	2X1	12/12	19X1	2X2	1+0	√169
225/15	3X4	√361	196/14	3X3	19-18	26-4
21/3	3X3	17-5	12+4	√361	324/18	3X2

WORDS

1. COUSINS
2. WIRED
3. FAMILY
4. MARKERS

EASY

3X3	19X1	15/3	6+6	3X3	√289	324/18
17-5	2X1	12-8	36/3	23X1	3X7	√441
25/25	36/6	1+0	22/22	144/12	√169	2X1
√9	√400	40/4	√324	14/2	4+1	20-18
2X2	3+4	24-23	√361	28-14	50-25	36-18
42/3	25/5	11+4	3X3	40-20	11+12	10+10
√100	√484	441/21	14-7	2X7	19X1	1X1

WORDS

1. WARNING
2. TASTY
3. UMBRELLA
4. BUILDS

EASY

15/3	3X1	√16	18-12	√144	196/14	2X1
5+4	4+2	18-9	25/5	38-19	30-12	2X2
12/3	35/5	5X1	√400	√121	5X1	81/9
√36	√144	16/4	30-15	5+6	25/5	324/18
21-3	20-11	√225	3X1	√324	3+2	30-16
30-14	15/3	3X3	144/12	18-9	19X1	12/12
225/15	324/18	3X2	15+4	√256	16-7	22-9

WORDS

1. LOOKERS
2. PICKER
3. FIELD
4. RESTED

EASY

19-2	225/15	2X3	14+4	√144	36-18	28-14
36-18	4+5	√441	√361	25/5	10+2	√324
484/22	12+2	10+10	5X1	7X1	35/7	18-9
45/5	3X2	2X7	30-11	38-19	2X7	2X1
6+7	4+3	13/13	3+2	10+5	26-13	5X3
5X4	√81	2+3	3X5	4+3	16/8	2X1
√225	256/16	√169	1+0	24-12	√100	12+12

WORDS

1. LOOSEN
2. IMAGES
3. RINGER
4. BELLS

EASY

90/5	2X3	15+8	21-3	√256	25/5	225/15
3+4	14/14	15-3	8+7	46-23	12/4	44-22
28-14	34-22	14+5	2X2	20-12	8+7	√49
36/12	2+10	27-18	11+8	5X1	√324	1+2
4+5	15/3	441/21	√400	2+3	22-20	4X2
8X3	24-7	225/15	10+10	3X6	36-18	3+2
324/18	57/3	64/8	√361	1X1	10-5	76/4

WORDS

1. SOULS
2. BREATH
3. CHEER
4. CROWDS

EASY

14-3	2X4	15+4	21-7	14+4	81/9	225/15
3X4	5+3	12+12	√256	10+10	38-19	45-30
√144	196/14	√81	6+7	24-12	12/12	√484
√625	676/26	√400	30-25	5X1	19-18	144/12
39/3	20/20	45-42	15/3	18-9	42/3	5X4
20-10	√225	45-34	6/2	38-19	√16	56-45
56/7	4X3	12+2	5X1	2+2	16-4	10-3

WORDS

1. DICED
2. PIECES
3. OATMEAL
4. OVALS

EASY

144/12	60/4	3X4	11+4	36-18	10+10	√361
2X2	√169	14+1	289/17	3X3	20-5	9X1
3X3	2+3	10+5	361/19	144/12	15/3	10-7
36/6	36/4	2X4	30-9	60/5	3X5	3X3
5+4	14-7	19X1	100/20	5+2	√441	42/3
39/3	15/3	3X7	5X1	28-14	1X1	√324
√225	256/16	√441	225/15	4X3	4+6	16-5

WORDS

1. ENOUGH
2. COURAGE
3. ROLLS
4. MOUSE

EASY

15-14	2X7	14+3	10+10	72/8	√144	169/13
24/8	3X3	11+2	2X7	12-7	√256	14-5
30-25	4X3	4+3	27/9	√324	19X1	√169
√625	361/19	1X1	225/15	3X2	1X1	20-2
14/14	2+3	4+7	30-12	45-35	5X1	30/10
8+7	11-5	19-5	24-23	12/6	14-11	3+2
3X1	3X5	26-13	2X7	56-55	14+4	√289

WORDS

1. BRACES
2. MAJOR
3. CAREER
4. CAMPING

EASY

12/12	169/13	4X3	19X1	5+7	12-9	12/4
28/14	44-22	5X1	26-20	36-18	3X5	46-23
2X3	2X7	6+6	3X7	30-15	7+7	10+3
√225	3+1	4+1	24-12	225/15	324/18	12+8
4X3	13+4	30-11	√400	√625	10+4	289/17
5X3	6-3	14/14	40-20	3X3	10+10	90/5
42/3	57/3	√256	20-5	21-20	225/15	4X4

WORDS

1. ATTENDS
2. POINT
3. CONTROL
4. YOURSELF

EASY

3X2	15-4	26-14	7+4	14/2	22/11	2+2
√324	3X4	1X1	28-14	3+2	22-19	3X3
39/3	√400	42/6	10+2	30-12	√324	√121
144/12	42-21	√25	2X4	18-9	60/5	4X5
3X6	√361	225/15	16/4	√121	2X1	18-9
19X1	400/20	2X8	1+0	10+9	38-19	30-12
30-14	4X3	4+1	30/5	√25	√1	2X1

WORDS

1. SPEAKS
2. CRIBS
3. RELATED
4. TOUGH

EASY

14-3	32-15	5X3	16-8	19X1	10+10	324/18
√289	11+3	5-4	√144	12/12	15-3	10-7
3X4	√81	5X1	3X3	2+2	42-21	√25
90/5	19X1	60/4	3X1	144/12	√16	7X1
4+3	38-19	30-18	25-24	36/12	12+10	1+0
4+1	324/18	√256	√25	3X3	2X7	26-13
15+4	3X1	√441	324/18	4+3	56/56	5+6

WORDS

1. SPECIAL
2. CUDDLE
3. CURLS
4. MANAGE

EASY

10-2	15/15	30-12	3X1	256/16	45/9	3X1
21+3	5X1	2+1	10+2	2X9	√400	14-5
361/19	10+2	30-11	√441	√225	3+2	2X1
4X2	25/5	1+0	2X2	√121	169/13	5+4
4+4	√576	4+1	3+2	√441	8+8	38-19
16-8	17-8	3+9	24-10	3+2	√196	10-2
15/15	3X4	15+4	144/12	19X1	30-12	484/22

WORDS

1. TOKENS
2. SPELLED
3. NUMBER
4. RELAXES

EASY

2X1	15-4	18-9	4X5	4+3	12+1	10+10
17-8	√529	√225	64/8	144/12	4+1	56-43
46/2	3X4	25/5	2X9	18-9	2X2	2X1
√324	361/19	1X1	√49	6+3	45/3	3X1
√121	2X1	400/20	26/2	72/6	24-12	14/14
3X5	15/5	16-8	4+1	25/25	√144	196/14
6+5	17-8	19X1	√576	3+1	3X1	3+2

WORDS

1. CLIMAX
2. HEATED
3. WORLD
4. GLOBE

EASY

45-33	3X4	8+6	4+4	16-4	225/15	32-16
28-14	46-23	5X1	12+9	2+1	4X5	144/12
√81	324/18	30-12	3X6	30-11	1X1	√169
40-36	40-20	√441	3X1	12+8	√400	√196
36/12	3X3	√196	10+10	3+2	2+1	12+5
60-48	50/10	8+7	361/19	100/20	100/10	√144
225/15	3+5	36/6	36-18	√256	2X3	2X1

WORDS

1. FENCES
2. PROTECT
3. PLANTS
4. NURTURE

EASY

2X2	15-4	15-8	12+7	3X3	256/16	90/5
57/3	3X3	39/3	√144	40-20	√529	676/26
26-13	√324	19X1	√361	36-18	12/12	20/4
30-16	5X1	441/21	47-34	1X1	60/5	12X1
12X2	38-19	2X1	1-0	3+2	2X2	2+1
√49	5+4	14+5	√256	108/9	15+3	14+8
21/3	√25	361/19	7X3	15/5	3X1	64/8

WORDS

1. PEARLS
2. RUBIES
3. CLEATS
4. CLASSES

EASY

√225	36/12	3X3	42-21	72/9	√81	√9
15/3	21/7	15/15	2X1	2X7	1X1	15/15
4+3	15-4	225/15	√324	27-18	26-13	19X1
25-8	3X4	25-21	√484	25/5	14+7	3+2
√484	10/2	6+6	5X1	6+7	30-11	625/25
441/21	25/5	2+2	3X3	324/18	√4	1X1
4+5	√25	√49	√196	28/14	2X3	28-14

WORDS

1. MINDED
2. UNIVERSE
3. COLLEGE
4. CAMERA

EASY

96-74	2X4	20/4	324/18	√361	225/15	2X1
17+2	3X6	45/3	12+8	28-14	25/5	20/5
√36	42/6	2X4	2+1	100/20	4+3	√361
10+9	3X2	35/5	2+2	3X3	22-17	2/2
25/1	5+4	38-19	72/8	30-16	√25	76/4
√121	32/4	529/23	√36	57/3	√441	46-23
56-34	67-56	3X5	30-12	3X4	12-7	8+9

WORDS

1. FIGHTER
2. SEEDS
3. UNICORN
4. HORSES

EASY

144/12	5+4	16-5	√196	25/5	2X2	63-54
35/5	√16	18-9	2X10	56/8	14-13	12+2
3X4	121/11	25/5	14/14	14+4	2X7	89-78
100/5	√1	36/2	30-12	3X4	4+2	14+3
42/3	1+0	2X1	57/3	4+1	15/15	90/5
3+2	4X4	3X1	√16	√400	64/8	56-51
63/7	3X7	21-5	57/3	14+5	1X1	10+10

WORDS

1. BAKING
2. AFRAID
3. SCARED
4. EATER

EASY

38-19	√225	2X2	40/5	81/9	12-8	42/6
4+2	√324	100/10	√25	2+1	36/6	√25
25-10	45/5	2X8	48/3	12+2	5+4	√400
√225	19X1	√225	48-32	2X3	3X7	15-4
3X5	3X4	8+7	√49	45/3	361/19	76/4
8+6	19X1	42/7	30-14	39/3	4X3	225/15
√625	484/22	26/2	24-20	3X2	10+10	15/3

WORDS

1. POISON
2. SUICIDE
3. MOPPED
4. FLOORS

EASY

28-14	2X2	15+6	18/2	30-14	48-24	13+2
√289	19X1	√1	3X5	6X2	256/16	2X1
√400	10+8	48-36	√441	5X1	√324	√169
4+4	72/8	2X9	1-0	8X2	3+2	30-12
3X2	12/3	3+2	6+7	4X5	50/10	3X5
14-8	18-9	12+8	15+4	42-21	10/5	√400
324/18	30-15	35-25	3X4	225/15	√361	32-19

WORDS

1. POURED
2. METALS
3. TRAILER
4. BUMPER

EASY

√64	4+3	√49	15-4	19X1	100/10	2X10
√121	63/7	28-14	20-2	108/9	4+4	15-4
36/6	4+3	27/3	3X2	√225	√324	484/22
44/11	2X4	1X1	√324	529/23	2X2	9+9
18-9	20-10	15/3	39/3	2X10	30/6	4X5
36-18	2X1	5X1	5+3	12/12	1X1	16/4
3X5	36-18	30-16	30-17	√144	2X7	28-10

WORDS

1. HIGHER
2. GROWTH
3. REMAIN
4. REALM

EASY

21/3	24/6	4+1	2X9	96-84	2+2	16-7
√361	22-11	√121	3X5	14/7	√144	35-30
57/19	5X1	108/9	19X1	√169	16/16	42/3
48/16	36-18	1X1	√25	95/5	3X2	10+3
10-9	√529	10+2	15/1	23-10	2X1	25-6
√529	2X1	√625	32/16	676/26	3X4	8X1
2X8	15+5	36/4	3+2	10/5	14-5	8+7

WORDS

1. WALKER
2. SMOKER
3. SMALL
4. BIBLE

EASY

3X4	3X5	15-4	32/2	36/9	20-10	18-9
14+3	3+2	1+0	2X7	14+5	√225	4X3
2X1	12+2	64/8	42-21	14-2	28-14	35/7
40/5	33-25	√225	√361	√1	60-48	11/11
54-36	19X1	2X2	324/18	3X3	3X1	361/19
√49	4+1	169/13	30-12	39-26	14+5	16/2
2X10	√196	3X3	4+5	1X1	3+2	3X5

WORDS

    1. MISHAPS
    2. SOUND
    3. ALARMED
    4. HEARING

EASY

12-3	3+2	3X4	441/21	2X2	196/14	21/7
4+5	12+12	12-9	30/15	10+8	12+8	3X5
√36	√121	11+2	12-11	10+4	√441	√1
24/2	55/5	25-20	10+10	√400	42/3	45-36
18-9	2X1	18-9	33-28	15-4	24-19	2X7
14/2	20-10	2X10	√324	72/9	√225	√196
13+4	30-12	19X1	√9	2X9	3X3	10+10

WORDS

1. TABLE
2. KITCHEN
3. COUNTER
4. CURTAIN

EASY

2X10	38-19	√25	3X3	60-48	√4	32-16
100/10	24-12	6+6	12-7	121/11	1+1	√324
3X4	6/3	√361	18/9	3X7	256/16	5X1
5X1	1X1	36-18	2+1	15+5	1X1	12/12
20/4	√4	15/5	100/20	42/6	32/8	3X2
1+3	12+6	5X1	3X1	1X1	3+2	√49
56/7	12/6	1+0	√81	√196	√225	3X3

WORDS

    1. BUBBLE
    2. CABLE
    3. DANCER
    4. BARBELL

EASY

10+10	43-35	√625	2X3	4X5	17-12	18/2
√25	√1	30-11	√361	625/25	4X3	12+12
26-13	361/19	2+2	1X1	15-12	2X1	30/5
2X3	5X1	3X3	√225	√25	15-10	3X3
√100	36-24	30-18	10+8	22-11	42/7	50/2
10-2	18-9	2X2	3X5	3X6	3+2	35/5
42/6	40/10	√400	441/21	24/3	√441	2X4

WORDS

1. CORDLESS
2. FEAST
3. HOLIDAY
4. TURKEY

EASY

2X4	15-10	30-11	25-10	38/2	3X3	10+10
√361	√441	√529	5-1	14-3	45-30	2X1
196/14	14+5	10+5	3X5	22/11	3X1	2X7
9X3	5X1	5X5	9+4	9/3	27-18	30-15
5X1	225/15	30-18	20/4	√1	3X3	√25
√625	√100	2X1	1X1	28-14	√361	12-5
19-12	4X3	30-17	12+2	15+4	6+3	15-12

WORDS

   1. JOYOUS
   2. OCCASION
   3. MALES
   4. WOMEN

EASY

12-3	36/12	3X2	90/5	15-3	√324	72-65
24-2	√144	3+2	1-0	√25	80/10	90/10
3X4	27-18	15-4	96/8	30-16	50-25	4X3
14+3	12/4	3X1	√9	3+2	10+8	20+2
10+10	√121	1X1	23-5	√256	√16	√361
√400	55-50	16+2	40-20	5X1	√400	2X1
12+12	3X4	2X2	√256	56/7	42/6	48/16

WORDS

1. DRYER
2. CARPET
3. CLEANER
4. CLICKED

EASY

12-3	3X3	35/5	√1	√81	27/9	10+10
15/3	1+1	√9	√144	42-21	3X1	14/2
11+3	22-11	5X1	1X1	√361	35-15	√324
361/19	25/5	16-12	225/15	4+5	3+2	3X3
20/10	2X2	√441	36-24	3X2	26-13	12+4
16/2	2X7	38-19	4+3	625/25	√81	19X1
30-12	22-1	2+2	14-2	28-14	132/11	√169

WORDS

1. FOUND
2. TIMING
3. GLADLY
4. BECAUSE

EASY

19X1	10+12	55-34	81/9	3X1	√81	√121
3X3	36-18	2X2	√49	54/6	30-16	5+2
4+5	12/3	12/12	2+2	15/3	√196	14-7
12-6	√25	11+8	3X4	45-30	18-9	5+3
4X5	30-9	10-5	2X3	30-15	12+1	39/3
√169	√81	6X2	3X3	2X4	3X3	56/7
√64	25/5	30/2	16/8	15-10	1+0	3X2

WORDS

1. USAGE
2. HOLDING
3. BLEED
4. AIMING

EASY

225/15	√324	2X2	4+1	√529	14+4	25-10
2X1	√256	35-15	81/9	√361	20-6	12+12
24/6	72/8	1X1	2X7	3X5	72/8	4+3
√121	√81	28-14	8/2	20/5	3X4	15-4
12/4	√36	3+2	4+5	2X9	12/3	21/7
3X2	42/6	√25	30-12	49/7	50/25	√64
√324	19X1	2X10	4-2	12-7	18-9	9/3

WORDS

1. WINNER
2. PADDING
3. BRIEF
4. CLOSET

EASY

46-23	36-18	2X2	15-6	96/8	15+3	2X5
225/15	40/5	30/6	4+4	21/3	25/5	23-12
52-26	324/18	2X1	3+4	3+2	√121	38-19
√169	28-23	3X4	√441	√676	√289	10+10
42/3	√144	36-20	10/2	2X5	14+7	21-16
15/5	3X4	361/19	3X3	100/20	2+1	5+5
√225	289/17	18-9	35/7	3X6	3X3	19X1

WORDS

1. JUGGLE
2. PIERCE
3. REBELS
4. SQUEEZE

EASY

3X1	15/5	25/5	12-6	√1	24/4	3+2
√400	15+7	√225	7+6	2X9	30-12	45-34
√324	14+4	8/2	361/19	5X1	√324	√169
19X1	1+0	3X3	3+2	11+3	15/3	3+2
30-14	12+2	√196	13+13	3X2	90/5	10+8
108/9	14-7	96-84	12+7	√25	5X3	14+3
√256	√484	3X4	19-2	12+3	15/4	24/6

WORDS

    1. FREEZER
    2. CODING
    3. TRANSFER
    4. FARMER

EASY

2X1	15+4	28-19	19X1	2X1	√361	15/15
45/9	30-11	38-19	81/9	√400	2X6	484/22
55/5	4+3	108/9	3X6	30-16	2X10	1X1
2X1	225/15	42-21	3+2	√256	1X1	39/3
144/12	30-12	√256	18/3	√1	√9	√81
5+4	16-8	3X2	17-3	15/3	30-16	17-4
4X3	15/3	225/15	30/5	4X3	√289	10/10

WORDS

1. FURNACE
2. SLEPT
3. FROGS
4. ANIMALS

EASY

10+3	144/12	3X1	3X2	15+4	6+7	100/10
√81	90-78	√144	5X3	√324	√225	361/19
19X1	54-45	3+2	21/7	√400	2X10	45-25
28-14	4+3	15/3	28-14	2X4	√1	42/3
39/3	10+9	324/18	2+3	1-0	16/8	6+6
38/2	144/12	16/16	12-7	√289	√169	25-6
3+3	19X1	19-12	441/21	1+1	10+10	14/14

WORDS

1. CHAMBERS
2. CLIENT
3. TOTALS
4. EQUALS

EASY

4+5	√361	57/3	19X1	484/22	3X3	625/25
5X5	100/20	10+10	5+5	14X1	4X4	8+8
64/8	√324	60/5	30-15	√49	324/18	√256
63/7	3+2	2X1	3+2	10/2	3X5	14-2
2X3	13X1	√64	32-16	1X1	11+12	15+5
4+6	12-7	169/13	9/3	5+7	12/4	15/3
36/6	√49	14+4	13+8	48/6	4X3	5+8

WORDS

1. PLUMMER
2. PREACHER
3. JOBLESS
4. TOPPING

EASY

√676	4X5	1+1	3X4	15/3	225/15	18-9
3X3	30-12	√25	3+2	25-6	13-8	12-8
24/2	√400	√81	14+5	√289	2X2	90/5
361/19	4/2	3X4	12+2	38-19	8+7	17-6
14-12	1X1	3X5	37-14	45/9	26-13	√324
32/2	16-4	8-6	2X1	√324	2X2	3+2
√36	132/11	15-14	16/16	√225	14+4	√64

WORDS

1. DESSERT
2. BABIES
3. ARMORED
4. LABORER

EASY

42/6	3X3	36-18	15+6	21-7	3X4	11+10
√225	32-22	45/5	20/4	3X1	25-7	4X5
7X1	15+10	√484	49/7	1X1	4X5	14+3
27-10	1X1	3X3	28-14	19X1	18-9	3X5
11X2	10-5	30-12	13-12	√9	5X1	44/11
5X1	529/23	√256	26-13	25/5	132/11	√256
√324	361/19	30-11	45-34	10+6	30-15	3X1

WORDS

1. REVIEW
2. TRANCE
3. SAMPLE
4. SPRAY

EASY

√144	225/15	2X4	15-5	30/6	42/3	15+5
400/20	3X4	11+1	√196	2X9	5+3	3+2
10/5	3+2	18-9	3X1	42/6	1X1	35/5
42/3	132/11	39/3	2X4	2X1	38-19	28-14
48/3	15-4	25-5	4X5	225/15	72/8	√25
100/20	√441	√225	√400	484/22	50/2	46-23
25/5	30-16	10+4	4X3	√1	29-10	2X8

WORDS

1. BOTTLE
2. ERASE
3. NOTHING
4. SAYING

EASY

25-5	144/12	169/13	2X7	3X1	18-9	2X10
16/2	3+2	2X8	45/3	4X4	14+3	30-12
6+7	9+1	√169	√324	12+12	10+10	3X7
√25	26-13	√4	√625	3X7	√324	42-40
42-21	14+7	3X5	20-11	2X9	9+7	6/3
14+3	40-20	15/5	3+4	2X7	14-9	3X3
1X1	3X1	22-11	14-7	26-13	28-12	3X2

WORDS

1. COMMON
2. PURPLE
3. TUBING
4. RUBBER

EASY

√121	3X4	26-13	15+4	35-20	81/9	√36
√25	256/16	19-18	10+10	√144	2X7	30-17
4X4	1X1	3X3	5X5	√225	42-21	2X2
25/5	√361	√256	18-9	3X5	10+10	44-22
√441	7X1	76/4	144/12	36-18	46-23	42-21
144/12	56/7	10+4	10-5	1-0	19X1	5X4
32-10	23X1	25/5	4+5	44-22	5X1	√625

WORDS

1. MULTIPLE
2. WAVING
3. PASSION
4. MAYORS

EASY

57/3	2X3	81/9	20-11	2X2	2X10	14-5
√324	49/7	225/15	54/6	2X7	1-0	56/7
4+3	30-11	12-2	√36	12+8	36-18	90/5
2X10	6+3	2X7	25/5	30-15	√25	√144
3-2	√121	1+1	√81	4X3	3X6	√324
18-2	50-16	2X2	196/14	35/7	1+1	30-16
10+10	3+2	14-5	11-6	7X1	5+6	√441

WORDS

1. BEFORE
2. PAINING
3. INTERN
4. RADIOS

EASY

√361	2X11	15+4	484/22	15/5	361/19	2X10
32-16	11+8	400/20	2X5	20-5	3X5	15-4
12+12	√196	144/12	2X4	5+4	3X4	24-1
3X5	√400	14-7	75/5	√169	3X5	4+1
3+4	324/18	5+3	28-14	42-21	10+5	2X2
12-6	√81	6+6	3+4	3X3	32/8	12+4
√81	72/8	64/8	2X2	15+4	25-7	22X1

WORDS

1. THOUGHT
2. WOODING
3. COILED
4. IRONS

EASY

14/14	36-18	38-20	34-14	2X10	2X7	5X1
34-23	3+2	3X4	5X1	14+4	3+2	90/5
√324	63/7	2X2	√196	√484	25/5	√64
81/9	1X1	75-60	24-12	2+2	12-7	9/3
20/4	15/3	2+1	√225	1+0	√64	√324
18-9	23X1	4+5	14+4	12-6	16+3	30-14
30-16	2X4	√81	√36	3X5	15+5	20-9

WORDS

1. FOLDER
2. CHARCOIL
3. NEVER
4. RENDER

EASY

72/8	20-15	2X10	√324	3X4	√625	12+12
26/13	72/4	3X1	√81	14/14	4X1	132/11
10+10	14-13	10+4	√16	44-22	3X3	√324
√16	3+2	√256	√25	10+8	1/1	3+4
14+4	16/16	60/5	1X2	5X1	14+4	20/5
32-16	20+5	1X1	√361	40-20	36-18	√49
√36	7X1	15/5	45-34	5X1	10+12	2X2

WORDS

    1. SERVICE
    2. APART
    3. DAILY
    4. CALENDAR

EASY

32-16	2X4	4X5	10/5	√25	2X2	15+5
35-10	16-8	32-25	32-16	3X4	90-72	√441
√16	6+6	√400	30/6	√484	12/6	81/9
15+10	15-10	5X1	28-14	72/9	25/5	8X2
14-3	√121	2X2	3X5	132/11	2X4	144/12
225/15	72/8	23X1	18-14	169/13	63/7	5+4
3+1	2X1	14-13	3X8	2X7	19+2	9X2

WORDS

1. MONTHLY
2. BEHIND
3. KEEPER
4. ABIDED

EASY

38-19	12-7	19-14	16-12	48/3	39-26	2X3
25/5	√144	44-22	2+3	3X5	10+10	12-3
18/2	38-19	3+2	48/3	7+5	100/20	3X3
108/9	30-16	√256	√81	14-9	√25	1+1
√324	√25	1X1	√121	√196	3X4	15+5
30-20	17-9	30-8	225/15	1X2	30-14	2X10
4+5	16+3	56/7	3X3	2X9	45/9	√361

WORDS

1. BELIEVE
2. HAPPEN
3. PROVEN
4. MODELS

EASY

2X3	16-5	56/8	2X1	√25	225/15	10+10
√324	19/19	√361	2X7	16-14	1X1	32-17
72/6	6+7	4X5	3+2	20/2	16/2	4X2
3X3	2+2	18-9	26-13	38-19	12/4	36-18
12+12	12+10	625/25	8+6	7X1	√64	15/3
2X2	√324	3X3	20-6	4+3	35/7	30/6
90/5	√196	√25	12+8	1-0	√144	3X1

WORDS

1. LIVING
2. ENEMY
3. CHEATER
4. GAMING

EASY

23-4	15/3	2X2	4+4	√121	400/20	2+1
19/19	100/10	441/21	√324	2X5	25/5	16-4
2X4	3X5	12/12	28-14	14+5	22-17	√225
√289	√625	3X3	2+3	7X1	10+2	30-12
324/18	19X1	3X4	10+4	19X1	16-12	30-15
4X2	42/6	3X6	25/5	30-11	√81	35/7
3X3	4+4	√196	225/15	√16	9+9	72/9

WORDS

1. LESSON
2. DRAINED
3. OLDER
4. YOUNGER

EASY

3X1	3X4	12+2	144/12	4X5	√441	625/25
25-6	30-12	1X1	400/20	11+11	38/2	57/3
55/11	24-20	11+8	2+3	4+5	5+6	42/6
√100	3+1	√225	10+8	30-16	28/2	14-13
2X1	3+3	324/18	45/3	√4	24/6	22/11
√49	√36	56/7	63/63	12/4	1+0	5X1
67-45	55-35	3X2	√49	1X1	44-24	4X1

WORDS

1. BREAD
2. BACON
3. FROSTING
4. GATED

EASY

√1	64/8	16-5	12+11	√529	3X3	144/12
16+7	30-16	32/2	4X3	30/2	42/3	39/3
7+6	5+6	3X3	169/13	33-30	3+1	2X8
45-34	33/11	24/2	5+6	2X7	√81	3X1
√441	38/2	60/5	108/9	√64	63/7	2X4
√36	10+5	3+2	19X1	30-15	57/3	46-23
36/12	30-14	√529	23-19	3X4	14+7	28/2

WORDS

    1. PICKLES
    2. PILLOWS
    3. WINDOW
    4. SHOULD

EASY

76/4	13+8	19-12	5X3	√289	256/16	3X3
√9	16/4	√400	10+12	441/21	√361	2+1
39-29	30/5	√225	√81	64/8	5X2	32/4
8-6	3X3	30-7	8+6	4+1	5X1	56-45
64-56	15-1	8+4	30-18	4+3	19-18	5X4
√676	529/23	3X4	2X6	14+7	40/10	√484
3X7	12+3	361/19	225/15	12/12	50/2	100/10

WORDS

1. SHELLS
2. DOWNLOAD
3. HEAVY
4. LIFTING

EASY

225/15	4X4	55/11	90/5	√121	2X10	15-4
8X2	7X1	42-21	19X1	30-12	25-24	18/1
6+7	2X7	√196	225/15	3X1	13+2	3+2
√324	12+8	6+3	67-45	√9	15/5	45-33
81/9	96/8	√4	√121	1+0	1-0	√25
324/18	2X1	1X1	15+10	√256	46-23	38-19
16/4	24/8	529/23	57/3	5X1	30-12	√289

WORDS

1. WAKING
2. RECAPS
3. LAWYERS
4. ACCOUNT

EASY

60/4	2+0	96/8	25-20	35/5	5+4	21-4
14+5	19+4	30-11	11/11	√25	256/16	√441
484/22	2X10	√196	20-6	2X9	10+10	1X1
12+12	20+5	3+2	45/5	√441	169/13	10+10
√196	42/6	√324	√169	361/19	76/4	45/5
3X3	7+7	26-13	√121	2+2	1X1	10/2
14-1	3X4	15/3	6+3	16/4	15+8	8X1

WORDS

1. SUNNY
2. ADMIRE
3. MIDWEST
4. EASTERN

EASY

3X4	14/7	√625	5X4	49/7	√225	76/4
39/3	36-18	√400	6+7	38/2	3X1	2X9
100/10	5X1	39/3	10+9	√324	5+3	484/22
90/18	36-18	1X1	25/5	4X4	√225	16/4
55/11	8+7	28/2	3X6	35-12	10+5	19-12
55-36	14+5	42/6	10+8	√144	√400	25/25
361/19	2X8	2X2	56/7	1-0	√529	4+3

WORDS

    1. WESTERN
    2. SCHOOL
    3. GRAMMY
    4. AWARDS

EASY

2+0	30-14	56-34	56/8	56/8	81/9	2X2
√25	36/12	3+2	3X5	24-12	34/2	60-40
225/15	√196	11+8	√196	576/24	36-27	36-18
46-23	3+4	256/16	√1	2+1	√49	12/12
15/3	10/5	√25	√324	13+1	15+5	2X2
64/8	√121	400/20	144/12	25-6	27-18	√169
400/20	3X1	15-4	18-9	28-14	30/2	30/5

WORDS

1. ARTIST
2. GOSPEL
3. TRADING
4. PENCIL

EASY

$\sqrt{324}$	35/5	3X4	144/12	$\sqrt{225}$	40-20	46-23
18/2	$\sqrt{25}$	3X3	19X1	12/6	$\sqrt{81}$	36/9
2X2	$\sqrt{1}$	3X4	15-10	1+0	9+7	$\sqrt{16}$
42/3	4X5	14-7	$\sqrt{144}$	2X7	36-24	76/4
90/5	42/3	3+2	60-48	1X1	45/3	3X6
2+2	324/18	81/9	15/15	$\sqrt{625}$	30-22	$\sqrt{256}$
45/5	40/5	3-1	16+3	2X9	20/4	12-10

WORDS

1. SINGLE
2. PLAYER
3. BALLER
4. PHONES

EASY

4X4	√441	10+9	484/22	22/11	√361	4+5
15+8	17-4	324/18	18/2	42/3	5X1	3X7
42-21	5X1	4+3	10/2	44-22	15-12	12-7
3X1	√64	4+4	3X3	√25	19X1	2X7
√324	400/20	30-11	28-14	196/14	10+10	√625
289/17	14+4	21-14	√441	72/8	25/5	5+1
12/2	6/2	3+4	4X1	12+12	√324	225/15

WORDS

1. USHERS
2. ENTERING
3. SEVEN
4. EIGHT

EASY

60/3	2X11	26-21	56-44	2X1	144/12	169/13
8+7	√121	14+5	√400	6+7	2X10	√25
4+3	5X1	13+2	1-0	√1	15+6	33-13
13X2	22-11	12+8	1+1	15-9	324/18	35/7
√64	√9	1X1	256/16	15/5	√324	56/8
72/8	3X6	3+2	6/2	√361	10+10	√196
324/18	3+5	15+5	10/2	36/2	4X6	√625

WORDS

1. BATTER
2. CAKES
3. SPECTATE
4. CRUMBLE

EASY

15+6	√196	24/2	49/7	55/5	3+4	144/12
√361	2X10	30-25	4+1	90/5	48/8	4X3
12-7	12+12	3+2	15/3	5X1	24/8	27-18
3X3	30-16	2X2	225/15	35/7	17/17	√324
361/19	√25	√144	12-11	14+9	16/4	√9
16/4	12+10	2X9	15/3	√441	√81	484/22
30/5	3X3	10-2	28-21	2X7	12/12	√361

WORDS

1. AWARE
2. NEEDLE
3. FEEDING
4. NESTLE

EASY

11+11	25-4	100/10	2X1	225/15	√361	84/12
3X4	15-10	19X1	2+3	24/8	3X4	27/9
32/16	2X2	14-7	30-11	1X1	1+0	4+4
√121	√441	14+6	33-19	√16	√25	18-9
10+4	3X6	25-6	5+4	63-54	10+8	2+1
10+10	2X1	46-23	3+2	20-15	√121	12/6
88/8	4+7	14-5	10+4	18-9	3X3	100/10

WORDS

    1. BREAST
    2. WINGS
    3. CHICKEN
    4. LADIES

EASY

2X2	60/20	4X4	√400	225/15	√324	1+1
10/2	19X1	14-9	27-22	√81	15+6	√324
441/21	2X4	√16	144/12	2X9	19/19	7X2
15+2	3+2	1X1	3X2	30/6	2+1	36/3
√144	20/4	72/6	100/20	11+8	20-11	121/11
√576	42/6	76-57	7+5	√9	64/8	34-21
76-54	89-76	39/3	28-14	4+1	48/3	10+10

WORDS

1. LEADER
2. LICENSE
3. SHELFS
4. BRACELET

EASY

24/2	15+5	625/25	√324	196/14	23X1	5+6
42/7	8+6	10+1	√400	√484	3X3	40-24
3+2	4X2	6X2	3X2	2+1	√49	√324
19X1	1+0	20-11	18-9	5+6	25-11	22-11
46/23	54-34	144/12	12/12	4+2	5+4	84/7
42/3	12+12	3X4	2X9	√529	√625	25/5
√324	361/19	256/16	30-15	38-19	5+4	12X1

WORDS

1. FIFTY
2. ALLOWING
3. PRICK
4. LIARS

EASY

2+0	169/13	35/5	32-12	3+2	√256	1X1
4+3	15/5	4X3	15-14	√289	3X1	72/6
12X2	4+3	10+10	4+5	√144	81/9	45/5
100/10	√196	3X6	2X10	361/19	√36	√256
19X1	5X1	27-18	225/15	12+7	3X5	4+2
8+6	30-11	√576	10+6	8+8	19-12	45-30
18/6	3X2	15+6	25-10	20/10	42-21	39/3

WORDS

1. PORTAL
2. POSTING
3. OFFICE
4. BOXES

EASY

√81	225/15	3X4	24/6	27-18	10+12	441/21
36/12	20/4	3X3	5+9	38/2	169/13	99/11
5+6	√196	12+12	√400	11/11	4X5	39-26
√441	10+5	30-6	√400	12-6	3X5	46-23
√289	√225	54/6	1X1	76/4	2+0	42/3
42/7	56/7	28-14	48-24	3+2	19X1	3X3
64/9	4+4	12-11	22-11	√25	108/9	45/5

WORDS

1. FAXES
2. EXXON
3. MOBILE
4. STATION

EASY

48-24	√49	√4	16/4	39-26	144/12	2X3
42/6	144/12	√256	25/5	64/8	√225	361/19
19X1	1+0	10+3	36/2	2X2	42/3	√121
2+2	3X7	42/6	57/3	90/18	2X7	84/7
25-20	42/3	30-14	4+4	6+3	20-7	12+8
10+6	19X1	√81	25-11	3X5	4+3	56/7
√484	529/23	1X1	10+10	√324	45-34	3X3

WORDS

1. PUMPED
2. MORNING
3. KNIGHT
4. GLADES

EASY

30/10	4+3	169/13	19X1	√196	60/4	45-31
32/16	35/7	2X2	√400	529/23	√225	63/9
3+2	7+7	144/12	3X4	1X1	12-8	10+8
√324	4+3	√324	14+5	324/18	3X6	361/19
10/2	3X3	14-9	33-28	4+1	4X5	√100
72/6	4X5	28-14	26-13	14/14	12+12	38-19
529/23	48-24	28-14	3X2	14+4	√676	55/11

WORDS

1. DREAMER
2. STARTS
3. ENGINE
4. GROWLS

EASY

14/2	25/5	3X5	17-2	3+2	144/12	√361
√169	23-10	35-16	3X3	√324	50/25	10/5
25-20	4X4	20/4	√9	2X4	5X1	11/11
45/5	6+7	22-17	441/21	√36	√400	48-24
46-23	2X1	√196	2X11	3X2	√484	81/9
64/8	25/5	3+2	20-1	2X4	12-7	√361
√36	19X1	36-18	49/7	3X1	10+10	4+3

WORDS

1. MEMBERS
2. EFFECTS
3. SCENES
4. BATHROOM

EASY

72/8	15/3	26-12	3X3	√144	99/9	225/15
80/20	3X4	100/20	40-22	9/3	√361	20/2
21/3	3X1	15+4	√81	√225	30-17	√100
39/3	2X9	76/4	2X7	3X1	16/8	5X1
90/5	√25	22-11	2X9	3X4	√121	2X9
4X4	12+9	2X2	50/2	3+2	30-11	14-9
√225	256/16	√49	√196	35/7	30-12	56/7

WORDS

1. BLENDER
2. ROCKER
3. JERSEY
4. KNICKS

EASY

1+1	225/15	√256	9X2	27-10	2X1	10+10
√529	2X2	√225	46-23	44-22	3X4	30-17
12+12	42/3	3+2	2X10	3+3	√25	14-7
28-14	5+6	15-10	2X2	57/3	1+0	84/7
72/6	14/14	12X2	144/12	3X5	12+2	4+5
64/8	√81	30-16	√4	5+4	2X1	√4
14/7	3X1	14-7	2X7	15/15	3X5	20/2

WORDS

1. BOSTON
2. NAKED
3. ABLED
4. MEANING

EASY

$\sqrt{576}$	90/30	3X3	10+1	$\sqrt{64}$	144/12	2X1
$\sqrt{324}$	361/19	10-5	96-84	2X8	2X10	4+3
42/6	36/2	$\sqrt{121}$	8+5	10+2	30-22	36-20
56-43	18-9	3X7	28-14	3X3	5+4	67-47
441/21	3X6	$\sqrt{484}$	$\sqrt{36}$	1+0	12-9	5X1
15/15	14-12	15+5	10/5	2X9	30-12	2X10
3+2	$\sqrt{289}$	256/16	2X3	256/16	$\sqrt{441}$	4X4

WORDS

1. FILLER
2. PRANK
3. PICTURE
4. TRIUMPH

EASY

12+12	√9	45/5	√361	2X1	100/10	√144
121/11	8+8	225/15	361/19	20-11	28-14	√324
90/18	15+4	2X7	42/6	5+4	1+1	4+3
3X3	2X10	√256	20-6	3+2	√1	√16
2X2	3+2	144/12	√196	4X5	10+4	√225
15-4	√196	1+0	29-20	1X1	15+6	3X1
7X3	4X4	40-20	29-10	3X1	12+2	22/11

WORDS

1. SPLIT
2. BANANA
3. SIGNING
4. CONTENT

EASY

90/30	3X1	2X8	15+4	3X4	3+2	38-19
3X7	484/22	1-0	12+8	√225	20-4	√625
√575	676/26	2X7	18-9	√16	3X5	90/5
39/3	2X1	15/3	14+4	3+2	19X1	√400
28/14	6/3	100/5	√81	25-9	10+10	30-14
256/16	35/5	7+7	54/6	27/3	2X8	81/9
13+13	4+5	25/5	√324	√144	169/13	4+5

WORDS

1. PAIRING
2. SPIRIT
3. SPOTTED
4. BENTLEY

EASY

42-21	30-11	2X5	10-9	14/2	25-19	5+2
225/15	√196	12-4	4X5	16-8	2X7	100/20
76/4	3X4	12/12	5X1	72/8	3+2	60/3
60/4	32/8	√324	1+0	√361	2X10	5X1
169/13	12-7	256/16	√144	4+4	√529	√576
6+9	33-28	30-16	3X3	45/9	4X3	15+10
66/11	3X1	42/3	12+12	2X1	2X2	24/6

WORDS

1. WHINED
2. HEALED
3. SHARPEN
4. TEXTING

EASY

84/7	3X4	15/5	5+3	256/16	√81	3X1
2X4	14-7	30-12	√25	3X1	35-15	2X11
441/21	35-30	30-11	3X5	√400	√196	16/8
46-23	28-14	√169	36-18	25-7	√441	55/11
39/3	90/5	324/18	1+1	19X1	12/12	2X1
14-13	3X5	√81	2X9	3+2	√121	24/8
324/18	√361	76/4	11+2	225/15	50/10	10/5

WORDS

1. MIRROR
2. USERS
3. EMBRACE
4. BENCHES

EASY

64/8	3+3	35/7	√25	12/3	46-23	4X5
√529	2X9	2X4	30-8	2+2	16-8	√361
48-24	13-2	14-11	3+2	8+7	1X1	√400
√121	1+0	144/12	3X1	10+10	48/3	196/14
225/15	400/20	100/20	5+6	5X1	18-9	18-5
19-1	2X7	84/7	2+1	3X6	30-12	√256
3X4	√196	√25	10/5	169/13	3X1	11+12

WORDS

1. BLEACHED
2. PERCENT
3. WHATEVER
4. PRINTS

EASY

$\sqrt{225}$	2X4	56/8	3X1	15-4	20/2	66/6
5+6	39/3	$\sqrt{64}$	$\sqrt{289}$	90/5	60/4	76/4
3X5	256/16	18-9	15/5	441/21	14+4	529/23
45-30	$\sqrt{144}$	67-57	5X1	4X3	11+11	72/8
$\sqrt{529}$	2X9	3+2	2X10	361/19	2X2	30-12
$\sqrt{100}$	45/9	256/16	169/13	$\sqrt{225}$	99/11	56-51
3X4	15-13	10+3	35-16	42-21	90/5	24/6

WORDS

1. SPEECH
2. IDIOT
3. LIQUOR
4. DRUMMER

EASY

1+1	144/12	3X1	3+2	15-4	45-25	60/4
10+10	18/6	16/2	2+2	√324	441/21	2X11
3+3	19X1	2X9	5X1	42/7	13+4	12+7
39-18	√1	√625	3X1	42/6	2X4	√121
8+7	46-23	2X1	30-11	√196	3X3	14+5
42/3	17-16	2X10	1-0	7+7	16/8	32/8
2X2	15-3	√144	1+0	6+6	√25	√256

WORDS

1. BANGED
2. CRYSTAL
3. SHINED
4. WASHER

EASY

2X2	20/4	√324	90/5	400/20	2X1	19-2
19X1	1X1	3+2	10+8	18-9	21/7	30-16
32/2	1X1	121/11	14-5	1-0	√196	√361
108/12	9X2	1X1	28-14	42/3	√49	49/7
27/3	100/20	15+4	√64	108/9	25/5	3+1
10+12	14+3	√361	1X1	38-19	√16	289/17
√484	441/21	2X1	19X1	19-14	4X3	14/2

WORDS

1. SHAKER
2. GLASSES
3. CANNED
4. EARRING

EASY

256/16	3X4	67-59	78-66	12+2	225/15	3X1
3X3	18-9	10+9	10/2	√441	48/3	3X2
4+5	10-5	5X5	5X1	3+1	12+12	12-11
38/2	30/6	24-12	361/19	56/7	26-13	√400
14+10	2X9	√25	2X2	24/8	√225	5X4
√81	72/9	5X1	√196	30/5	32/4	42/3
14+3	38-19	√1	44/11	17-4	77/11	16-8

WORDS

1. CHEESE
2. HANDLE
3. AMONG
4. DESIRE

EASY

144/12	2X1	45-30	√361	27-18	4X3	10+10
√361	441/21	48/3	33/3	10+10	42-21	3X1
72/9	32-20	√324	90/5	19X1	√196	10-1
√64	63/9	1X1	5X1	15/3	36-18	12+6
4+3	2X8	10+8	14+5	15-6	22-17	4+1
3X5	√361	25/25	57/3	3X3	529/23	√25
441/21	12/4	3+2	2X10	28-14	24/6	99/11

WORDS

1. GRACES
2. REINDEER
3. PRESENTS
4. SPARKS

EASY

36/4	3X1	14+6	28-19	3X3	√400	√144
225/15	√25	3+5	3+2	33-22	1X1	19-12
256/16	3X4	√256	7+5	26-13	√361	√4
√324	1+1	2X9	1X1	10+8	√1	30-24
67-59	40-30	60/4	1+0	16/2	3X5	46-23
44-22	30-12	12/12	625/25	2+1	76/4	676/26
3X2	13X2	5X1	324/18	2X2	4+5	10-4

WORDS

1. CHALKS
2. BOARDS
3. PRAYER
4. FORMAT

EASY

18/6	3+4	12+12	√16	√361	441/21	2X1
14+7	4X5	28-10	54-34	√225	21/7	5X1
14-3	2X9	√400	14-7	3X3	4+4	45/5
3X3	1+1	100/20	2X8	√1	2X7	10-9
14/14	√144	30/5	√324	8+7	4+3	15/3
225/15	17-12	42-21	√256	30-11	48/3	39/3
76/4	4X3	10+8	38-19	10+10	30-16	3X3

WORDS

1. CHAOS
2. REFERS
3. DOING
4. BLURP

EASY

100/10	13+5	48/3	43-29	56-45	4X3	13+3
256/16	25/5	14-7	√324	72/8	196/14	√225
4X3	45/9	√121	144/12	√529	3X1	√25
7+7	2X9	1+0	3+2	28-14	15+5	19X1
2+1	12+11	24/3	5X1	10+10	√361	10+10
72/9	90/18	√9	√81	2X1	3X5	28-14
46-23	3X1	15+4	19-11	18/3	3X2	225/15

WORDS

1. SNEAKER
2. CHEWING
3. BITTEN
4. WRENCH

EASY

169/13	$\sqrt{324}$	3+2	30-16	80-67	6X3	15-3
12X2	$\sqrt{256}$	25/5	$\sqrt{49}$	18-9	4X3	14+4
33/11	2X2	13+3	5+6	14-5	$\sqrt{16}$	$\sqrt{225}$
441/21	225/15	48/3	2X8	$\sqrt{1}$	10+4	361/19
10+10	13/13	$\sqrt{64}$	2+3	3X5	15-14	5+4
10+8	3X4	19X1	16-12	36-18	25-6	12-3
39/3	30-7	$\sqrt{324}$	676/26	19-17	4X5	14-10

WORDS

1. SOAKED
2. SHOPPER
3. BRANDING
4. WRAPPED

EASY

144/12	23X1	45/9	$\sqrt{361}$	$\sqrt{400}$	5+6	169/13
5+6	27/3	60/5	19X1	30-14	1-0	25-6
57/3	2X2	11+4	1X1	$\sqrt{441}$	3+2	5X1
256/16	225/15	3X4	676/26	$\sqrt{121}$	15-6	16-8
7-6	14-12	24/12	13X2	3X3	$\sqrt{25}$	$\sqrt{529}$
529/23	$\sqrt{441}$	25-11	$\sqrt{25}$	24-12	4+5	38/2
90/5	3X2	42/6	43-30	5+5	10+10	2X1

WORDS

1. PUZZLE
2. LAKES
3. BODIES
4. WHEATS

EASY

√1	2+3	10/5	144/12	90/5	20/5	2X9
4X6	3+1	3+2	√81	√25	45/9	41-35
22-10	√144	44-22	11+3	196/14	√25	2X10
14+5	3X5	4+5	2X9	24-21	42/6	19X1
√324	30-7	361/19	√324	42-21	1+0	18-5
15/3	28-14	3X2	2X2	3X4	√400	11+11
45/5	40/5	5X1	√9	121/11	2X8	2X4

WORDS

1. DRIVING
2. TURNED
3. NECKLACE
4. BELOW

EASY

34/2	36-18	2X2	10+10	√100	45-34	35-12
108-96	3X2	15/3	22-18	√225	√121	27-20
57/3	3X1	√324	5X1	42/3	38-19	2X7
10-9	2+1	3X8	20-16	4+5	3X3	√81
4+5	20-12	√1	18-9	√400	24/12	19-2
√289	32/8	2X11	361/19	256/16	12/12	15/5
16/4	2X3	5X1	√169	108/9	15+6	21/7

WORDS

1. BINDER
2. VIDEOS
3. CASTING
4. CALMED

EASY

19X1	45-34	3+4	32-16	5+3	24/6	4+3
√121	144/12	3X4	19X1	√256	14-13	3X5
50/2	100/20	3+2	50/10	56/4	27/3	3+2
14+4	1X1	5+6	√25	√49	√361	√324
√361	30-16	30-19	5X1	2X9	22/11	1+1
14/14	3+2	4+3	9+9	2X7	√400	36/9
√625	144/12	√64	81/9	6+7	4X3	15/3

WORDS

1. ANGER
2. ANGLES
3. RIPPLE
4. TREES

EASY

24/6	44/11	2X10	2+3	√256	3X5	10+10
√400	3+2	225/15	√441	7+7	2X10	3X4
15/1	36/2	46-23	4+5	32-16	35/5	121/11
12/12	√121	√225	56/7	8+5	√361	2X4
12+4	√144	28-14	15/5	225/15	13-8	5+6
8+7	√121	20-15	√9	√576	15/15	8/2
2X7	√256	42/3	57/19	100/20	19X1	2X10

WORDS

1. COMPUTER
2. KNOWING
3. DESKTOP
4. EXCEL

EASY

2X3	15-4	5+2	30-11	√529	√324	361/19
12+3	196/14	√144	8+7	4X5	26-10	3+4
16/4	14/14	72/8	30-12	√16	5+3	48/3
25/5	√400	42-21	3+2	38-19	√225	3X3
√529	1X1	6X4	46-23	324/18	16/2	15+4
3X7	21-13	√324	5X1	45/3	6+7	12+1
15/15	16-3	3+2	11+3	10+9	7+6	19-8

WORDS

1. SEXUAL
2. HORMONE
3. WORSHIP
4. RATINGS

ANSWERS

PAGE 7

			36/12=C (2)			
	√361=S (3)			36-18=R (2)		
		400/20=T (3)	1+0=A (2)		30-11=S (4)	
	25/5=E (3)		26-13=M (2)			2X6=L (4)
	1X1=A (3)	4X4=P (2)		19X1=S (1)	13-12=A (4)	√169=M (4)
		24-12=L (3)	3X5=O (1)	6+6=L (1)	10+5=O (4)	14+4=R (4)
		√144=L (1)	1X1=A (1)	45-42=C (1)		

PAGE 8

			36-24=L (1)	32/8=D (4)	√400=T (4)	
		25-24=A (1)	3+2=E (4)	2X9=R (4)		
	3X1=C (3)	√441=U (1)	8/4=B (3)	3+6=I (4)		
	25-10=O (3)	√169=M (3)	56/8=G (1)	38-19=S (3)	21/7=C (2)	3+1=D (2)
		2X4=H (1)		324/18=R (2)	5X1=E (2)	
				√81=I (2)		

					9/3=C (4)	
		√361=S (4)	14+5=S (4)	√324=R (4)		
		2+2=D (2)		225/15=O (4)	60/5=L (1)	40/10=D (3)
	3X4=L (2)	10+10=T (1)	2X4=H (1)	7+2=I (1)	5X1=E (3)	
	30-11=S (1)	5X1=E (2)	72/8=I (2)	√49=G (1)		30-16=N (3)
				√625=Y (2)	36-18=R (3)	
			12-10=B (3)	441/21=U (3)		

						24/12=B (3)
			19X1=S (2)			35/7=E (3)
			3X5=O (1)	4+3=G (2)	3+2=E (1)	√144=L (3)
		72/6=L (1)	2X7=N (2)	46-23=W (1)	√400=T (3)	10+8=R (1)
		45/5=I (2)	26/13=B (1)	5X1=E (3)	196/14=N (4)	√196=N (4)
		√361=S (2)	36-24=L (4)	81/9=I (4)	2+2=D (3)	32-27=E (4)

				7-2=E (1)		
	2X7=N (3)			$\sqrt{484}=V$ (1)		
		7X1=G (3)	1X1=A (1)	3X3=I (2)	100-88=L (1)	24-12=L (2)
		18-9=I (3)	12+8=T (2)	25/5=E (1)	144/12=L (2)	
		11+8=S (2)	9-4=E (3)	1X1=A (4)	$\sqrt{324}=R$ (4)	12/4=C (4)
		4+8=L (4)	$\sqrt{529}=W$ (4)	$\sqrt{324}=R$ (3)		

		2X2=D (4)	48/4=L (1)		14-7=G (2)	
		30-15=O (1)	25-20=E (4)			30-16=N (2)
		4+1=E (1)	12+10=V (1)	361/19=S (4)	3X3=I (2)	
	30-12=R (1)	7X1=G (3)	$\sqrt{225}=O$ (4)	$\sqrt{400}=T$ (3)	2X2=D (2)	42/6=G (2)
	18-9=I (3)	144/12=L (4)	64/8=H (3)	$\sqrt{81}=I$ (2)	49/7=G (2)	
	27/9=C (4)	10+9=S (3)				

PAGE 13

						√361=S (4)
		12-6=F (2)			√256=P (4)	
			1X1=A (2)			36-18=R (4)
		3X3=I (2)	5X1=E (2)	38-19=S (1)	1X1=A (4)	√484=V (1)
		24-12=L (2)	81/9=I (1)	16/4=D (2)	15-6=I (1)	√529=W (4)
		√196=N (3)	3X5=O (1)	3+2=E (3)		
	√121=K (3)		25/5=E (3)	2X7=N (1)	19X1=S (3)	

PAGE 14

					24/12=B (2)	36/6=F (3)
				46-23=W (3)	√441=U (2)	3X4=L (3)
		22-11=K (1)	20-6=N (3)		8+7=O (3)	40-20=T (2)
			81/9=I (1)	2X7=N (2)	15+5=T (2)	
		√400=T (1)	5+4=I (4)	5X1=E (1)	√225=O (2)	
		2X1=B (4)	12+8=T (1)	324/18=R (4)	11+3=N (1)	
			3+2=E (4)		√400=T (4)	

		30-12=R (3)				√324=R (2)	
		2X2=D (4)	5+4=I (3)			18-9=I (2)	
529/23=W (1)		3+2=E (4)	3X2=F (3)	7X1=G (2)		1+4=E (4)	42/7=F (4)
	12+6=R (1)	96/8=L (3)	324/18=R (4)	1X1=A (4)		64/8=H (2)	
		3X3=I (1)	25/5=E (3)	5X1=E (1)		√400=T (2)	
			40-20=T (1)				

		26-13=M (4)		√169=M (2)		
		7+2=I (4)	1X1=A (2)			
	19X1=S (4)		√81=I (2)			
		38-19=S (4)	225/15=O (1)	4+8=L (2)	19X1=S (3)	144/12=L (3)
	25/5=E (4)	23-3=T (1)	10-5=E (2)	√49=G (1)	63/7=I (3)	3+2=E (3)
	√361=S (4)	10+10=T (1)		16-12=D (2)		√121=K (3)
			5X1=E (1)	2X7=N (1)		

			√625=Y (3)			
		20-8=L (3)		√400=T (1)	36-18=R (4)	
	12+8=T (3)		64/8=H (1)			5/1=E (4)
		361/19=S (3)	√49=G (2)	3X3=I (1)	4X4=P (4)	4+3=G (2)
		√225=O (3)	28-14=N (1)	2X7=N (2)	30-15=O (2)	2X8=P (4)
		56/8=G (1)	√169=M (3)	18-9=I (2)	441/21=U (4)	
		19X1=S (1)				

PAGE 18

	256/16=P (4)					
		50/10=E (4)	2X7=N (2)		√529=W (3)	
	3+2=E (4)	35/7=E (2)	36-18=R (1)			3+2=E (3)
	8+8=P (4)	2X2=D (2)	25/5=E (1)		19-18=A (3)	
	19X1=S (4)	32-16=P (1)	24-12=L (2)	11+4=O (1)	30-14=P (3)	
		225/15=O (2)	√256=P (1)	3X5=O (3)	√9=C (1)	
			14-7=G (2)	10+4=N (3)	√361=S (3)	

				38-19=S (4)		
		20/10=B (2)	10-5=E (4)		√441=U (4)	72/9=H (3)
		36-18=R (3)	1X1=A (2)	√256=P (3)	1X1=A (3)	√225=O (4)
		4+3=G (2)	3+2=E (3)	56/8=G (2)	√169=M (3)	16-8=H (4)
		√49=G (2)	25/25=A (2)	46-23=W (1)	5X1=E (2)	
			5X1=E (1)	361/19=S (1)		
			16/4=D (1)	3+2=E (1)		

				√324=R (4)	38-19=S (4)	
			5X1=E (4)	√49=G (3)		
		√169=M (1)	20/4=E (3)	√121=K (4)	3+2=E (3)	42/6=G (2)
		28-14=N (3)	225/15=O (1)	1X1=A (4)	64/8=H (2)	144/12=L (3)
	2X2=D (3)	19X1=S (1)	√484=V (1)	26-13=M (4)	45-30=O (2)	
			3+2=E (1)	18-9=I (1)	12+7=S (2)	
						√400=T (2)

			20-8=L (1)	11-10=A (4)			
		25-20=E (1)	2X10=T (4)	4/2=B (1)	√25=E (4)		
		4+1=E (4)	36/3=L (3)	169/13=M (1)	10+8=R (4)	√361=S (3)	
		√36=F (2)	14+4=R (3)	√441=U (1)	√529=W (3)	1+2=C (4)	
		5X1=E (2)	81/9=I (2)	3X3=I (3)	16-8=H (1)		
	2X2=D (2)	30-12=R (2)					

			√324=R (1)	1+2=C (2)			
			3X3=I (2)	30-15=O (1)	5X1=E (2)		
			√169=M (1)	40-20=T (2)	10+5=O (3)		
	16/4=D (4)	1X1=A (1)		√529=W (3)	√225=O (2)	3X4=L (3)	
	√225=O (4)	2X7=N (1)		√16=D (4)	√196=N (2)	144/12=L (3)	
	30-10=T (4)	9/3=C (1)	3+2=E (4)		20/4=E (3)		
	25/5=E (1)	4X5=T (4)		√625=Y (3)			

PAGE 23

		√324=R (1)				2X2=D (3)
		10+9=S (4)	25/5=E (1)		√25=E (3)	
	3X3=I (4)	19X1=S (2)	32-16=P (4)	√81=I (1)		40-20=T (3)
	2X4=H (4)	1X1=A (1)	4+3=G (2)	72/9=H (1)	1+0=A (3)	54/9=F (2)
	1+2=C (1)	√529=W (4)	38-19=S (1)	2X7=N (2)	144/12=L (2)	2+2=D (3)
				3X3=I (2)		

PAGE 24

			12+8=T (1)			
		2X9=R (1)		3X5=O (4)	225/15=O (4)	
		3+6=I (1)	2X9=R (4)	30-11=S (2)	24-12=L (4)	6/2=C (4)
			32-16=P (1)	19X1=S (4)	15+5=T (2)	2X2=D (2)
	2+2=D (3)	√225=O (3)	144/12=L (1)	3X3=I (2)	√81=I (2)	
		2+3=E (1)	√441=U (3)	10-5=E (3)	49/7=G (2)	
				2X1=B (3)	24-12=L (3)	

			12+8=T (4)	25-20=E (4)	√441=U (4)	
			20-11=I (2)	√256=P (1)	49/7=G (2)	√289=Q (4)
		√400=T (2)	25/5=E (1)	2X7=N (2)	√361=S (1)	20-6=N (4)
		45/9=E (2)	5X1=E (1)		1X1=A (4)	
		36-18=R (1)	10-5=E (2)	40/20=B (4)	64/8=H (3)	45/45=A (3)
		6+7=M (2)	2+1=C (1)	5X1=E (3)	4+3=G (3)	34-14=T (3)
				√324=R (3)		

		5X1=E (4)				26-13=M (4)
	10+8=R (4)	46-23=W (2)	√121=K (4)	5X5=Y (3)	1X1=A (4)	
	19X1=S (4)	12-3=I (2)		3X6=R (4)	24-12=L (3)	9-6=C (1)
		√324=R (2)	3+2=E (2)	30-9=U (1)	√225=O (1)	81/9=I (3)
			19X1=S (1)	2X2=D (2)		√169=M (3)
		√361=S (1)	196/14=N (1)	3X3=I (1)	19-18=A (3)	
						3X2=F (3)

	19X1=S (4)		6+6=L (4)	3X3=I (4)	
		12-8=D (4)	36/3=L (3)	23X1=W (1)	3X7=U (4)	√441=U (3)
		1+0=A (3)	22/22=A (1)	144/12=L (3)	√169=M (3)	2X1=B (4)
√400=T (2)		√324=R (1)		4+1=E (3)	20-18=B (3)
	24-23=A (2)	√361=S (2)	28-14=N (1)	50-25=Y (2)	36-18=R (3)
		3X3=I (1)	40-20=T (2)		
		14-7=G (1)	2X7=N (1)		

		√16=D (4)	18-12=F (3)			
		18-9=I (3)	25/5=E (4)	38-19=S (4)	30-12=R (4)	
		5X1=E (3)	√400=T (4)	√121=K (1)	5X1=E (4)	
	√144=L (3)	16/4=D (3)	30-15=O (1)	5+6=K (2)	25/5=E (1)	324/18=R (2)
		√225=O (1)	3X1=C (2)	√324=R (1)	3+2=E (2)	
			144/12=L (1)	18-9=I (2)	19X1=S (1)	
				√256=P (2)		

					√144=L (4)	36-18=R (3)	
			√361=S (4)	25/5=E (3)	10+2=L (4)	√324=R (3)	
			5X1=E (1)	7X1=G (3)	35/7=E (4)	18-9=I (3)	
		2X7=N (1)	30-11=S (2)	38-19=S (1)	2X7=N (3)	2X1=B (4)	
			3+2=E (2)	10+5=O (1)			
	√81=I (2)		3X5=O (1)	4+3=G (2)			
		√169=M (2)	1+0=A (2)	24-12=L (1)			

PAGE 30

					46-23=W (4)	12/4=C (3)	
		14+5=S (1)	2X2=D (4)	20-12=H (3)	8+7=O (4)		
	2+10=L (1)		11+8=S (4)	5X1=E (3)	√324=R (4)	1+2=C (4)	
		441/21=U (1)		2+3=E (3)	22-20=B (2)		
		225/15=O (1)	10+10=T (2)	3X6=R (2)	36-18=R (3)		
		64/8=H (2)	√361=S (1)	1X1=A (2)	10-5=E (2)		

PAGE 31

			√256=P (2)		38-19=S (4)	45-30=O (4)
		√81=I (2)	6+7=M (3)	24-12=L (4)	12/12=A (3)	√484=V (4)
		√400=T (3)	30-25=E (2)	5X1=E (3)	19-18=A (4)	144/12=L (3)
	20/20=A (3)	45-42=C (2)	15/3=E (2)	18-9=I (1)		
	√225=O (3)		6/2=C (1)	38-19=S (2)	√16=D (1)	
			5X1=E (1)	2+2=D (1)		

PAGE 32

				36-18=R (3)		
	√169=M (4)				20-5=O (3)	
		10+5=O (4)	361/19=S (3)	144/12=L (3)		10-7=C (2)
		2X4=H (1)	30-9=U (4)	60/5=L (3)	3X5=O (2)	
	14-7=G (1)	19X1=S (4)	100/20=E (1)	5+2=G (2)	√441=U (2)	
	15/3=E (4)	3X7=U (1)	5X1=E (2)	28-14=N (1)	1X1=A (2)	√324=R (2)
			225/15=O (1)			

PAGE 33

				72/8=I (4)			
			2X7=N (4)	12-7=E (1)	√256=P (4)		
		4+3=G (4)	27/9=C (1)	√324=R (2)	19X1=S (1)	√169=M (4)	
		1X1=A (1)	225/15=O (2)		1X1=A (4)	20-2=R (3)	
			30-12=R (1)	45-35=J (2)	5X1=E (3)	30/10=C (4)	
			24-23=A (2)	12/6=B (1)	14-11=C (3)	3+2=E (3)	
	26-13=M (2)			56-55=A (3)	14+4=R (3)		

PAGE 34

			19X1=S (4)				12/4=C (3)
		5X1=E (4)	26-20=F (4)	36-18=R (4)	3X5=O (3)		
	2X7=N (1)	6+6=L (4)	3X7=U (4)	30-15=O (3)	7+7=N (3)		
	3+1=D (1)	4+1=E (1)	24-12=L (3)	225/15=O (4)	324/18=R (3)	12+8=T (3)	
		30-11=S (1)	√400=T (1)	√625=Y (4)	10+4=N (2)		
			40-20=T (1)	3X3=I (2)	10+10=T (2)		
		√256=P (2)	20-5=O (2)	21-20=A (1)			

		1X1=A (3)		3+2=E (3)	22-19=C (2)		
	√400=T (3)	42/6=G (4)	10+2=L (3)	30-12=R (2)	√324=R (3)		
	42-21=U (4)	√25=E (3)	2X4=H (4)	18-9=I (2)			
	√361=S (1)	225/15=O (4)	16/4=D (3)	√121=K (1)	2X1=B (2)		
	400/20=T (4)	2X8=P (1)	1+0=A (1)	10+9=S (2)	38-19=S (1)		
		4+1=E (1)					

			√144=L (2)			10-7=C (2)
		5X1=E (2)		2+2=D (2)	42-21=U (2)	√25=E (4)
	19X1=S (3)			144/12=L (1)	√16=D (2)	7X1=G (4)
	38-19=S (1)	30-18=L (3)	25-24=A (1)	36/12=C (1)		1+0=A (4)
	324/18=R (3)	√256=P (1)	√25=E (1)	3X3=I (1)	2X7=N (4)	26-13=M (4)
	3X1=C (3)	√441=U (3)			56/56=A (4)	

PAGE 37

		30-12=R (4)				
	5X1=E (4)			2X9=R (3)	√400=T (1)	
	10+2=L (4)	30-11=S (4)		√225=O (1)	3+2=E (3)	2X1=B (3)
	25/5=E (4)	1+0=A (4)	2X2=D (2)	√121=K (1)	169/13=M (3)	
	√576=X (4)	4+1=E (2)	3+2=E (1)	√441=U (3)	8+8=P (2)	38-19=S (2)
		3+9=L (2)	24-10=N (1)	3+2=E (2)	√196=N (3)	
			144/12=L (2)	19X1=S (1)		

PAGE 38

	√529=W (3)	√225=O (3)	64/8=H (2)	144/12=L (3)	4+1=E (4)	
		25/5=E (2)	2X9=R (3)		2X2=D (3)	2X1=B (4)
		1X1=A (2)	√49=G (4)	6+3=I (1)	45/3=O (4)	3X1=C (1)
		400/20=T (2)	26/2=M (1)	72/6=L (4)	24-12=L (1)	
			4+1=E (2)	25/25=A (1)		
			√576=X (1)	3+1=D (2)		

PAGE 39

		8+6=N (4)				32-16=P (3)
		5X1=E (4)	12+9=U (4)			144/12=L (3)
		30-12=R (4)	3X6=R (4)	30-11=S (3)	1X1=A (3)	
	40-20=T (4)	√441=U (4)	3X1=C (1)	12+8=T (2)	√400=T (3)	√196=N (3)
		√196=N (1)	10+10=T (2)	3+2=E (1)	2+1=C (2)	
	50/10=E (1)	8+7=O (2)	361/19=S (1)	100/20=E (2)		
		36/6=F (1)	36-18=R (2)	√256=P (2)		

PAGE 40

			12+7=S (1)			
			√144=L (1)	40-20=T (3)		
	√324=R (2)	19X1=S (4)	√361=S (3)	36-18=R (1)	12/12=A (3)	20/4=E (3)
	5X1=E (4)	441/21=U (2)		1X1=A (1)	60/5=L (3)	
	38-19=S (4)	2X1=B (2)	1-0=A (4)	3+2=E (1)		2+1=C (3)
	5+4=I (2)	14+5=S (4)	√256=P (1)	108/9=L (4)		
	√25=E (2)	361/19=S (2)		15/5=C (4)		

PAGE 41

			42-21=U (2)			√9=C (4)
	21/7=C (3)	15/15=A (4)		2X7=N (2)	1X1=A (4)	
		225/15=O (3)	√324=R (4)	27-18=I (2)	26-13=M (4)	
	3X4=L (3)	25-21=D (1)	√484=V (2)	25/5=E (4)		3+2=E (2)
	10/2=E (1)	6+6=L (3)	5X1=E (2)	6+7=M (1)	30-11=S (2)	
	25/5=E (3)	2+2=D (1)	3X3=I (1)	324/18=R (2)		
	√25=E (3)	√49=G (3)	√196=N (1)			

PAGE 42

		20/4=E (1)	324/18=R (3)			
	3X6=R (1)	45/3=O (3)	12+8=T (1)	28-14=N (3)		
		2X4=H (1)	2+1=C (3)	100/20=E (2)		√361=S (2)
		35/5=G (1)	2+2=D (2)	3X3=I (3)	22-17=E (2)	
		38-19=S (2)	72/8=I (1)	30-16=N (3)	√25=E (4)	76/4=S (4)
	32/4=H (4)		√36=F (1)	57/3=S (4)	√441=U (3)	
		3X5=O (4)	30-12=R (4)			

			√196=N (1)		2X2=D (2)	63-54=I (2)
	√16=D (3)	18-9=I (1)		56/8=G (1)	14-13=A (2)	
	121/11=K (1)	25/5=E (3)		14+4=R (2)		
	√1=A (1)	36/2=R (3)	30-12=R (4)		4+2=F (2)	
	1+0=A (3)	2X1=B (1)		4+1=E (4)	15/15=A (2)	
		3X1=C (3)		√400=T (4)		56-51=E (4)
			57/3=S (3)		1X1=A (4)	

38-19=S (4)		2X2=D (3)		81/9=I (2)	12-8=D (2)	
	√324=R (4)		√25=E (3)	2+1=C (2)		√25=E (2)
25-10=O (4)	45/5=I (1)	2X8=P (3)	48/3=P (1)		5+4=I (2)	
√225=O (4)	19X1=S (1)	√225=O (1)	48-32=P (3)		3X7=U (2)	
3X5=O (1)	3X4=L (4)			45/3=O (3)		76/4=S (2)
8+6=N (1)		42/7=F (4)		39/3=M (3)		

PAGE 45

			18/2=I (3)	30-14=P (1)			
	19X1=S (2)	√1=A (3)	3X5=O (1)	6X2=L (3)			
√400=T (3)	10+8=R (3)	48-36=L (2)	√441=U (1)	5X1=E (3)	√324=R (3)	√169=M (2)	
		2X9=R (1)	1-0=A (2)	8X2=P (4)	3+2=E (2)	30-12=R (4)	
	12/3=D (1)	3+2=E (1)	6+7=M (4)	4X5=T (2)	50/10=E (4)		
				42-21=U (4)	10/5=B (4)		

PAGE 46

√64=H (1)		√49=G (2)				
	63/7=I (1)	28-14=N (3)	20-2=R (2)			
	4+3=G (1)	27/3=I (3)		√225=O (2)		
	2X4=H (1)	1X1=A (3)	√324=R (1)	529/23=W (2)		9+9=R (4)
		15/3=E (1)	39/3=M (3)	2X10=T (2)	30/6=E (4)	
		5X1=E (3)	5+3=H (2)		1X1=A (4)	
	36-18=R (3)		30-17=M (4)	√144=L (4)		

PAGE 47

		4+1=E (1)	2X9=R (1)	96-84=L (3)		
	22-11=K (1)	√121=K (2)	3X5=O (2)		√144=L (3)	
	5X1=E (2)	108/9=L (1)		√169=M (2)	16/16=A (3)	
	36-18=R (2)	1X1=A (1)	√25=E (4)	95/5=S (2)		10+3=M (3)
	√529=W (1)	10+2=L (4)				25-6=S (3)
	2X1=B (4)		32/16=B (4)			
		36/4=I (4)				

PAGE 48

			32/2=P (1)	36/9=D (2)		
		1+0=A (1)	2X7=N (2)	14+5=S (1)		
		64/8=H (1)	42-21=U (2)			
		√225=O (2)	√361=S (1)	√1=A (3)	60-48=L (3)	11/11=A (3)
	19X1=S (2)	2X2=D (3)	324/18=R (3)	3X3=I (1)		
√49=G (4)	4+1=E (3)	169/13=M (3)	30-12=R (4)	39-26=M (1)		16/2=H (4)
	√196=N (4)	3X3=I (4)		1X1=A (4)	3+2=E (4)	

	3+2=E (1)	3X4=L (1)	441/21=U (4)			21/7=C (3)
		12-9=C (4)	30/15=B (1)	10+8=R (4)	12+8=T (4)	3X5=O (3)
			12-11=A (1)	10+4=N (3)	√441=U (3)	√1=A (4)
	55/5=K (2)		10+10=T (3)	√400=T (1)	42/3=N (2)	45-36=I (4)
		18-9=I (2)	33-28=E (3)		24-19=E (2)	2X7=N (4)
	2X10=T (2)	√324=R (3)	72/9=H (2)			
			√9=C (2)			

		√25=E (2)		60-48=L (1)	√4=B (1)		
	24-12=L (4)	6+6=L (2)	12-7=E (1)		1+1=B (1)		
3X4=L (4)	6/3=B (2)		18/9=B (1)	3X7=U (1)			
5X1=E (4)	1X1=A (2)	36-18=R (3)					
	√4=B (4)	15/5=C (2)	100/20=E (3)		32/8=D (3)		
	12+6=R (4)		3X1=C (3)	1X1=A (3)			
	12/6=B (4)	1+0=A (4)		√196=N (3)			

PAGE 51

		√625=Y (3)		4X5=T (2)		
	√1=A (3)	30-11=S (1)	√361=S (2)			
	361/19=S (1)	2+2=D (3)	1X1=A (2)	15-12=C (1)		
	5X1=E (1)	3X3=I (3)	√225=O (1)	√25=E (2)		
	36-24=L (1)	30-18=L (3)	10+8=R (1)	22-11=K (4)	42/7=F (2)	50/2=Y (4)
		2X2=D (1)	3X5=O (3)	3X6=R (4)	3+2=E (4)	
		√400=T (4)	441/21=U (4)	24/3=H (3)		

PAGE 52

		30-11=S (1)				
	√441=U (1)	√529=W (4)			45-30=O (2)	
	14+5=S (3)	10+5=O (1)	3X5=O (4)		3X1=C (2)	2X7=N (2)
	5X1=E (3)	5X5=Y (1)	9+4=M (4)	9/3=C (2)		30-15=O (2)
	225/15=O (1)	30-18=L (3)	20/4=E (4)	√1=A (2)	3X3=I (2)	
	√100=J (1)		1X1=A (3)	28-14=N (4)	√361=S (2)	
		30-17=M (3)				

PAGE 53

	36/12=C (4)		90/5=R (1)			
	√144=L (4)	3+2=E (3)	1-0=A (3)	√25=E (1)		
	27-18=I (4)		96/8=L (3)	30-16=N (3)	50-25=Y (1)	
	12/4=C (2)	3X1=C (4)	√9=C (3)	3+2=E (3)	10+8=R (1)	
	√121=K (4)	1X1=A (2)	23-5=R (3)		√16=D (1)	
	55-50=E (4)	16+2=R (2)		5X1=E (2)	√400=T (2)	
		2X2=D (4)	√256=P (2)			

PAGE 54

		35/5=G (3)	√1=A (4)			
	1+1=B (4)	√9=C (4)	√144=L (3)	42-21=U (4)		
		5X1=E (4)	1X1=A (3)	√361=S (4)	35-15=T (2)	
		16-12=D (3)	225/15=O (1)		3+2=E (4)	3X3=I (2)
		√441=U (1)	36-24=L (3)	3X2=F (1)	26-13=M (2)	
	2X7=N (1)		4+3=G (2)	625/25=Y (3)	√81=I (2)	
		2+2=D (1)		28-14=N (2)		

				√49=G (1)	54/6=I (2)	30-16=N (2)	5+2=G (4)
		12/3=D (3)	12/12=A (1)	2+2=D (2)	15/3=E (1)	√196=N (4)	14-7=G (2)
		√25=E (3)	11+8=S (1)	3X4=L (2)		18-9=I (4)	
		30-9=U (1)	10-5=E (3)		30-15=O (2)		39/3=M (4)
			6X2=L (3)		2X4=H (2)	3X3=I (4)	
				16/8=B (3)		1+0=A (4)	

				4+1=E (4)	√529=W (1)		
		√256=P (2)	35-15=T (4)	81/9=I (1)	√361=S (4)	20-6=N (2)	
			1X1=A (2)	2X7=N (1)	3X5=O (4)	72/8=I (2)	4+3=G (2)
			28-14=N (1)	8/2=D (2)	20/5=D (2)	3X4=L (4)	
		√36=F (3)	3+2=E (1)	4+5=I (3)	2X9=R (3)		21/7=C (4)
			√25=E (3)	30-12=R (1)		50/25=B (3)	

	36-18=R (3)			96/8=L (1)			
		30/6=E (3)		21/3=G (1)	25/5=E (1)		
		2X1=B (3)	3+4=G (1)	3+2=E (4)			38-19=S (4)
	28-23=E (3)		√441=U (1)	√676=Z (4)	√289=Q (4)		
	√144=L (3)	36-20=P (2)	10/2=E (4)	2X5=J (1)	14+7=U (4)	21-16=E (2)	
		361/19=S (3)	3X3=I (2)	100/20=E (4)	2+1=C (2)		
			35/7=E (2)	3X6=R (2)			

	15/5=C (2)		12-6=F (4)	√1=A (4)	24/4=F (1)	
√400=T (3)		√225=O (2)		2X9=R (1)	30-12=R (4)	
	14+4=R (3)	8/2=D (2)		5X1=E (1)	√324=R (3)	√169=M (4)
	1+0=A (3)	3X3=I (2)	3+2=E (1)		15/3=E (3)	3+2=E (4)
	12+2=N (2)	√196=N (3)	13+13=Z (1)	3X2=F (3)	90/5=R (1)	10+8=R (4)
	14-7=G (2)		12+7=S (3)	√25=E (1)		

				$\sqrt{361}$=S (4)	
30-11=S (2)	38-19=S (3)			2X6=L (4)	
4+3=G (3)	108/9=L (2)	3X6=R (1)	30-16=N (1)	2X10=T (2)	1X1=A (4)
225/15=O (3)	42-21=U (1)	3+2=E (2)	$\sqrt{256}$=P (2)	1X1=A (1)	39/3=M (4)
30-12=R (3)		18/3=F (1)	$\sqrt{1}$=A (4)	$\sqrt{9}$=C (1)	$\sqrt{81}$=I (4)
	3X2=F (3)		15/3=E (1)	30-16=N (4)	

		3X1=C (2)			
		$\sqrt{144}$=L (2)		$\sqrt{225}$=O (3)	
54-45=I (2)		21/7=C (1)	$\sqrt{400}$=T (2)	2X10=T (3)	45-25=T (3)
	15/3=E (2)	28-14=N (2)	2X4=H (1)	$\sqrt{1}$=A (3)	
10+9=S (1)	324/18=R (1)	2+3=E (4)	1-0=A (1)		6+6=L (3)
144/12=L (4)	16/16=A (4)	12-7=E (1)	$\sqrt{289}$=Q (4)	$\sqrt{169}$=M (1)	25-6=S (3)
19X1=S (4)		441/21=U (4)	1+1=B (1)		

		57/3=S (3)	19X1=S (3)		3X3=I (4)	
	100/20=E (3)		5+5=J (3)	14X1=N (4)	4X4=P (2)	8+8=P (4)
	√324=R (1)	60/5=L (3)	30-15=O (3)	√49=G (4)	324/18=R (2)	√256=P (4)
	3+2=E (1)	2X1=B (3)		10/2=E (2)	3X5=O (4)	
	13X1=M (1)	√64=H (2)	32-16=P (1)	1X1=A (2)		15+5=T (4)
	12-7=E (2)	169/13=M (1)	9/3=C (2)	5+7=L (1)		
		14+4=R (2)	13+8=U (1)			

	30-12=R (1)	√25=E (1)	3+2=E (2)	25-6=S (2)	13-8=E (3)	
	√400=T (1)	√81=I (2)	14+5=S (1)		2X2=D (3)	90/5=R (3)
	4/2=B (2)			38-19=S (1)	8+7=O (3)	
	1X1=A (2)			45/9=E (1)	26-13=M (3)	√324=R (4)
		8-6=B (2)	2X1=B (4)	√324=R (3)	2X2=D (1)	3+2=E (4)
	132/11=L (4)	15-14=A (4)	16/16=A (3)	√225=O (4)	14+4=R (4)	

		36-18=R (1)				
			20/4=E (1)		25-7=R (2)	4X5=T (2)
	15+10=Y (4)	√484=V (1)		1X1=A (2)		
	1X1=A (4)	3X3=I (1)	28-14=N (2)	19X1=S (3)		
	10-5=E (1)	30-12=R (4)	13-12=A (3)	√9=C (2)	5X1=E (3)	
	529/23=W (1)	√256=P (4)	26-13=M (3)	25/5=E (2)	132/11=L (3)	
		30-11=S (4)		10+6=P (3)		

				30/6=E (2)		
			√196=N (3)	2X9=R (2)		
	3+2=E (1)	18-9=I (3)		42/6=G (3)	1X1=A (2)	35/5=G (4)
	132/11=L (1)		2X4=H (3)	2X1=B (1)	38-19=S (2)	28-14=N (4)
		25-5=T (1)	4X5=T (3)	225/15=O (1)	72/8=I (4)	√25=E (2)
		√225=O (3)	√400=T (1)		50/2=Y (4)	
		10+4=N (3)		√1=A (4)	29-10=S (4)	

PAGE 65

	144/12=L (2)		2X7=N (1)			
	3+2=E (2)	2X8=P (2)	45/3=O (1)			30-12=R (4)
		√169=M (1)	√324=R (2)			3X7=U (4)
	26-13=M (1)	√4=B (3)		3X7=U (2)		42-40=B (4)
	14+7=U (3)	3X5=O (1)	20-11=I (3)	2X9=R (4)	9+7=P (2)	6/3=B (4)
	40-20=T (3)	15/5=C (1)		2X7=N (3)	14-9=E (4)	
			14-7=G (3)			

PAGE 66

		26-13=M (4)				
	256/16=P (3)	19-18=A (4)	10+10=T (1)	√144=L (1)	2X7=N (3)	30-17=M (1)
	1X1=A (3)	3X3=I (1)	5X5=Y (4)	√225=O (3)	42-21=U (1)	
	√361=S (3)	√256=P (1)	18-9=I (3)	3X5=O (4)		
	7X1=G (2)	76/4=S (3)	144/12=L (1)	36-18=R (4)	46-23=W (2)	
		10+4=N (2)	10-5=E (1)	1-0=A (2)	19X1=S (4)	
			4+5=I (2)	44-22=V (2)		

			20-11=I (3)	2X2=D (4)		
		225/15=O (4)	54/6=I (4)	2X7=N (3)	1-0=A (4)	
	30-11=S (4)		√36=F (1)	12+8=T (3)		90/5=R (4)
	6+3=I (2)	2X7=N (2)	25/5=E (1)	30-15=O (1)	√25=E (3)	
3-2=A (2)		1+1=B (1)	√81=I (2)		3X6=R (1)	√324=R (3)
18-2=P (2)			196/14=N (2)	35/7=E (1)		30-16=N (3)
				7X1=G (2)		

				15/5=C (3)		
	11+8=S (4)	400/20=T (1)		20-5=O (3)		
	√196=N (4)		2X4=H (1)	5+4=I (3)	3X4=L (3)	24-1=W (2)
3X5=O (4)	√400=T (1)	14-7=G (2)	75/5=O (1)		3X5=O (2)	4+1=E (3)
	324/18=R (4)	5+3=H (1)	28-14=N (2)	42-21=U (1)	10+5=O (2)	2X2=D (3)
	√81=I (4)		3+4=G (1)		3X3=I (2)	32/8=D (2)

PAGE 69

	36-18=R (1)	38-20=R (4)			2X7=N (3)	
	3+2=E (1)	3X4=L (2)	5X1=E (4)		3+2=E (3)	90/5=R (4)
	63/7=I (2)	2X2=D (1)	√196=N (4)	√484=V (3)	25/5=E (4)	
		75-60=O (2)	24-12=L (1)	2+2=D (4)	12-7=E (3)	9/3=C (2)
		2+1=C (2)	√225=O (1)	1+0=A (2)	√64=H (2)	√324=R (3)
			14+4=R (2)	12-6=F (1)		

PAGE 70

	20-15=E (1)	2X10=T (2)	√324=R (4)		√625=Y (3)	
	72/4=R (2)	3X1=C (1)	√81=I (1)	14/14=A (4)		132/11=L (3)
	14-13=A (2)	10+4=N (4)	√16=D (4)	44-22=V (1)	3X3=I (3)	
	3+2=E (4)	√256=P (2)		10+8=R (1)	1/1=A (3)	
	16/16=A (2)	60/5=L (4)		5X1=E (1)		20/5=D (3)
		1X1=A (4)	√361=S (1)			
		15/5=C (4)				

				√25=E (3)		
	16-8=H (1)		32-16=P (3)		90-72=R (3)	
√16=D (4)	6+6=L (1)	√400=T (1)	30/6=E (3)		12/6=B (2)	
15+10=Y (1)	15-10=E (4)	5X1=E (3)	28-14=N (1)		25/5=E (2)	
	√121=K (3)	2X2=D (4)	3X5=O (1)		2X4=H (2)	
	72/8=I (4)		18-14=D (2)	169/13=M (1)	63/7=I (2)	
	2X1=B (4)	14-13=A (4)		2X7=N (2)		

	12-7=E (1)	19-14=E (4)	16-12=D (4)		39-26=M (4)	
	√144=L (4)	44-22=V (1)		3X5=O (4)		
	38-19=S (4)	3+2=E (1)	48/3=P (2)	7+5=L (1)	100/20=E (1)	
	30-16=N (3)	√256=P (2)	√81=I (1)	14-9=E (2)		1+1=B (1)
	√25=E (3)	1X1=A (2)		√196=N (2)		
	17-9=H (2)	30-8=V (3)	225/15=O (3)		30-14=P (3)	
				2X9=R (3)		

PAGE 73

		56/8=G (4)		√25=E (2)			
	19/19=A (4)		2X7=N (2)				
72/6=L (1)	6+7=M (4)		3+2=E (2)				
3X3=I (1)		18-9=I (4)	26-13=M (2)		12/4=C (3)		
	12+10=V (1)	625/25=Y (2)	8+6=N (4)	7X1=G (1)	√64=H (3)		
	√324=R (3)	3X3=I (1)	20-6=N (1)	4+3=G (4)	35/7=E (3)		
		√25=E (3)	12+8=T (3)	1-0=A (3)			

PAGE 74

		2X2=D (2)				
		441/21=U (4)	√324=R (2)			
	3X5=O (4)	12/12=A (2)	28-14=N (4)		22-17=E (4)	√225=O (3)
	√625=Y (4)	3X3=I (2)	2+3=E (1)	7X1=G (4)	10+2=L (3)	30-12=R (4)
		3X4=L (1)	10+4=N (2)	19X1=S (1)	16-12=D (3)	
			25/5=E (2)	30-11=S (1)		35/7=E (3)
		√196=N (1)	225/15=O (1)	√16=D (2)	9+9=R (3)	

PAGE 75

		1X1=A (1)	400/20=T (3)			
	24-20=D (1)	11+8=S (3)	2+3=E (1)	4+5=I (3)		42/6=G (3)
		√225=O (3)	10+8=R (1)	30-16=N (2)	28/2=N (3)	
		324/18=R (3)	45/3=O (2)	√4=B (1)	24/6=D (4)	22/11=B (2)
	√36=F (3)			12/4=C (2)	1+0=A (2)	5X1=E (4)
			√49=G (4)	1X1=A (4)	44-24=T (4)	

PAGE 76

			12+11=W (3)			
		32/2=P (2)		30/2=O (3)		
		3X3=I (2)		33-30=C (1)	3+1=D (3)	2X8=P (1)
		24/2=L (2)	5+6=K (1)	2X7=N (3)	√81=I (1)	
	38/2=S (1)	60/5=L (2)	108/9=L (1)	√64=H (4)	63/7=I (3)	
	10+5=O (2)	3+2=E (1)	19X1=S (2)	30-15=O (4)	57/3=S (4)	46-23=W (3)
		√529=W (2)	23-19=D (4)	3X4=L (4)	14+7=U (4)	

PAGE 77

	16/4=D (2)	√400=T (4)			√361=S (1)	
	30/5=F (4)	√225=O (2)	√81=I (4)	64/8=H (1)		32/4=H (3)
	3X3=I (4)	30-7=W (2)	8+6=N (4)	4+1=E (1)	5X1=E (3)	
	15-1=N (2)	8+4=L (4)	30-18=L (1)	4+3=G (4)	19-18=A (3)	
		3X4=L (2)	2X6=L (1)		40/10=D (2)	√484=V (3)
		361/19=S (1)	225/15=O (2)	12/12=A (2)	50/2=Y (3)	

PAGE 78

	7X1=G (1)	42-21=U (4)			25-24=A (4)	18/1=R (2)
	2X7=N (4)	√196=N (1)	225/15=O (4)	3X1=C (4)		3+2=E (2)
	12+8=T (4)	6+3=I (1)		√9=C (4)	15/5=C (2)	
	96/8=L (3)		√121=K (1)	1+0=A (1)	1-0=A (2)	
		1X1=A (3)	15+10=Y (3)	√256=P (2)	46-23=W (1)	38-19=S (3)
		529/23=W (3)	57/3=S (2)	5X1=E (3)	30-12=R (3)	

PAGE 79

			25-20=E (4)			
		30-11=S (4)	11/11=A (4)	√25=E (2)		
	2X10=T (4)	√196=N (1)	20-6=N (1)	2X9=R (2)		
	20+5=Y (1)	3+2=E (4)	45/5=I (2)	√441=U (1)		10+10=T (3)
		√324=R (4)	√169=M (2)	361/19=S (1)	76/4=S (3)	
	7+7=N (4)	26-13=M (3)		2+2=D (2)	1X1=A (2)	10/2=E (3)
			6+3=I (3)	16/4=D (3)	15+8=W (3)	

PAGE 80

		√625=Y (3)				76/4=S (2)
		√400=T (1)	6+7=M (3)		3X1=C (2)	
	5X1=E (1)	39/3=M (3)	10+9=S (1)		5+3=H (2)	
	36-18=R (1)	1X1=A (3)	25/5=E (1)		√225=O (2)	
		28/2=N (1)	3X6=R (3)	35-12=W (1)	10+5=O (2)	
	14+5=S (4)	42/6=G (3)	10+8=R (4)	√144=L (2)		25/25=A (4)
		2X2=D (4)		1-0=A (4)	√529=W (4)	

PAGE 81

	30-14=P (4)		56/8=G (2)			
		3+2=E (4)	3X5=O (2)	24-12=L (4)		60-40=T (3)
		11+8=S (2)	√196=N (4)		36-27=I (4)	36-18=R (3)
		256/16=P (2)	√1=A (1)	2+1=C (4)	√49=G (3)	12/12=A (3)
		√25=E (2)	√324=R (1)	13+1=N (3)	15+5=T (1)	2X2=D (3)
		400/20=T (1)	144/12=L (2)	25-6=S (1)	27-18=I (3)	
			18-9=I (1)			

PAGE 82

	√25=E (1)		19X1=S (4)	12/6=B (3)		
		3X4=L (1)	15-10=E (4)	1+0=A (3)	9+7=P (2)	
		14-7=G (1)	√144=L (3)	2X7=N (4)	36-24=L (2)	
	42/3=N (1)	3+2=E (3)	60-48=L (3)	1X1=A (2)	45/3=O (4)	
	324/18=R (3)	81/9=I (1)		√625=Y (2)	30-22=H (4)	√256=P (4)
			16+3=S (1)	2X9=R (2)	20/4=E (2)	

		10+9=S (1)			√361=S (3)	
		324/18=R (1)			5X1=E (3)	
	5X1=E (1)	4+3=G (4)	10/2=E (4)	44-22=V (3)		12-7=E (2)
	√64=H (4)	4+4=H (1)	3X3=I (4)	√25=E (3)		2X7=N (2)
	400/20=T (4)	30-11=S (1)	28-14=N (2)	196/14=N (3)	10+10=T (2)	
		21-14=G (2)	√441=U (1)	72/8=I (2)	25/5=E (2)	
					√324=R (2)	

		26-21=E (3)		2X1=B (4)	144/12=L (4)	
		14+5=S (2)	√400=T (3)	6+7=M (4)	2X10=T (1)	√25=E (4)
	5X1=E (2)		1-0=A (3)	√1=A (1)	15+6=U (4)	33-13=T (1)
	22-11=K (2)	12+8=T (3)	1+1=B (1)		324/18=R (4)	35/7=E (1)
	√9=C (3)	1X1=A (2)	256/16=P (3)	15/5=C (4)	√324=R (1)	
		3+2=E (3)	6/2=C (2)	√361=S (3)		

PAGE 85

	$\sqrt{196}$=N (2)	24/2=L (4)				
$\sqrt{361}$=S (4)	2X10=T (4)	30-25=E (2)	4+1=E (4)		48/8=F (3)	
12-7=E (4)		3+2=E (2)		5X1=E (3)		
	30-16=N (4)	2X2=D (2)		35/7=E (3)	17/17=A (1)	
	$\sqrt{25}$=E (1)	$\sqrt{144}$=L (2)	12-11=A (1)	14+9=W (1)	16/4=D (3)	
		2X9=R (1)	15/3=E (2)		$\sqrt{81}$=I (3)	
			28-21=G (3)	2X7=N (3)		

PAGE 86

		19X1=S (2)			3X4=L (4)	27/9=C (3)
		14-7=G (2)	30-11=S (1)	1X1=A (1)	1+0=A (4)	4+4=H (3)
		14+6=T (1)	33-19=N (2)	$\sqrt{16}$=D (4)	$\sqrt{25}$=E (1)	18-9=I (3)
		25-6=S (4)	5+4=I (2)	63-54=I (4)	10+8=R (1)	2+1=C (3)
		46-23=W (2)	3+2=E (4)	20-15=E (3)	$\sqrt{121}$=K (3)	12/6=B (1)
		10+4=N (3)				

		√400=T (4)			1+1=B (4)
19X1=S (3)	14-9=E (4)	27-22=E (1)			√324=R (4)
2X4=H (3)	√16=D (1)	144/12=L (4)	2X9=R (1)	19/19=A (4)	
3+2=E (3)	1X1=A (1)	3X2=F (3)	30/6=E (4)	2+1=C (4)	36/3=L (2)
20/4=E (2)	72/6=L (3)	100/20=E (1)	11+8=S (3)	20-11=I (2)	
	76-57=S (2)	7+5=L (1)	√9=C (2)		
		28-14=N (2)	4+1=E (2)		

		625/25=Y (1)			
		√400=T (1)		3X3=I (3)	40-24=P (3)
	6X2=L (4)	3X2=F (1)	2+1=C (3)	√49=G (2)	√324=R (3)
1+0=A (2)	20-11=I (4)	18-9=I (1)	5+6=K (3)	25-11=N (2)	
	144/12=L (2)	12/12=A (4)	4+2=F (1)	5+4=I (2)	
	3X4=L (2)	2X9=R (4)	√529=W (2)		
		30-15=O (2)	38-19=S (4)		

PAGE 89

				3+2=E (3)			
			15-14=A (1)		3X1=C (3)		
	4+3=G (2)	10+10=T (1)		√144=L (1)	81/9=I (3)		
	√196=N (2)	3X6=R (1)	2X10=T (2)		√36=F (3)	√256=P (2)	
	5X1=E (4)	27-18=I (2)	225/15=O (1)	12+7=S (2)	3X5=O (2)	4+2=F (3)	
	30-11=S (4)	√576=X (4)	10+6=P (1)			45-30=O (3)	
			25-10=O (4)	20/10=B (4)			

PAGE 90

	20/4=E (2)			38/2=S (4)			
	√196=N (4)	12+12=X (2)		11/11=A (4)	4X5=T (4)	39-26=M (3)	
	10+5=O (4)	30-6=X (2)	√400=T (4)	12-6=F (1)	3X5=O (3)		
	√225=O (2)	54/6=I (4)	1X1=A (1)		2+0=B (3)		
		28-14=N (2)	48-24=X (1)	3+2=E (3)	19X1=S (1)	3X3=I (3)	
				√25=E (1)	108/9=L (3)		

	√49=G (4)					
	144/12=L (4)	√256=P (1)	25/5=E (1)			
	1+0=A (4)	10+3=M (1)		2X2=D (1)		√121=K (3)
2+2=D (4)	3X7=U (1)	42/6=G (2)			2X7=N (3)	
25-20=E (4)	42/3=N (2)	30-14=P (1)		6+3=I (3)	20-7=M (2)	12+8=T (3)
	19X1=S (4)	√81=I (2)	25-11=N (2)	3X5=O (2)	4+3=G (3)	56/7=H (3)
				√324=R (2)		

			19X1=S (2)			
	35/7=E (3)		√400=T (2)	529/23=W (4)	√225=O (4)	63/9=G (4)
	7+7=N (3)		3X4=L (4)	1X1=A (2)	12-8=D (1)	10+8=R (4)
	4+3=G (3)	√324=R (1)	14+5=S (4)	324/18=R (2)	3X6=R (1)	
	3X3=I (3)	14-9=E (1)	33-28=E (3)	4+1=E (1)	4X5=T (2)	
		28-14=N (3)	26-13=M (1)	14/14=A (1)		38-19=S (2)

		3X5=O (4)	17-2=O (4)			
√169=M (1)	23-10=M (4)	35-16=S (3)		√324=R (4)		10/5=B (4)
25-20=E (1)			√9=C (3)	2X4=H (4)	5X1=E (2)	11/11=A (4)
	6+7=M (1)	22-17=E (3)		√36=F (2)	√400=T (4)	
	2X1=B (1)	√196=N (3)		3X2=F (2)		
	25/5=E (1)	3+2=E (3)	20-1=S (1)		12-7=E (2)	√361=S (2)
	19X1=S (3)	36-18=R (1)		3X1=C (2)	10+10=T (2)	

						99/9=K (4)	
				40-22=R (2)	9/3=C (4)	√361=S (4)	
				√81=I (4)	√225=O (2)		√100=J (3)
	2X9=R (1)			2X7=N (4)	3X1=C (2)	16/8=B (1)	5X1=E (3)
	√25=E (1)	22-11=K (4)			3X4=L (1)	√121=K (2)	2X9=R (3)
		2X2=D (1)	50/2=Y (3)	3+2=E (1)	30-11=S (3)	14-9=E (2)	
			√196=N (1)	35/7=E (3)	30-12=R (2)		

	2X2=D (2)	√225=O (1)				30-17=M (4)	
	42/3=N (1)	3+2=E (2)	2X10=T (1)		√25=E (4)		
	5+6=K (2)	15-10=E (3)	2X2=D (3)	57/3=S (1)	1+0=A (4)		
	14/14=A (2)		144/12=L (3)	3X5=O (1)	12+2=N (4)		
		30-16=N (2)	√4=B (3)	5+4=I (4)	2X1=B (1)		
		14-7=G (4)	2X7=N (4)	15/15=A (3)			

PAGE 96

				√64=H (4)		
		10-5=E (1)	96-84=L (1)	2X8=P (4)		
	36/2=R (1)	√121=K (2)	8+5=M (4)	10+2=L (1)		36-20=P (3)
	18-9=I (4)	3X7=U (4)	28-14=N (2)	3X3=I (1)	5+4=I (3)	
	3X6=R (4)		√36=F (1)	1+0=A (2)	12-9=C (3)	5X1=E (3)
		15+5=T (4)		2X9=R (2)	30-12=R (3)	2X10=T (3)
				256/16=P (2)	√441=U (3)	

PAGE 97

	√9=C (4)		√361=S (3)			
		225/15=O (4)		20-11=I (3)	28-14=N (3)	
	15+4=S (1)	2X7=N (4)	42/6=G (3)	5+4=I (3)	1+1=B (2)	4+3=G (3)
	2X10=T (4)	√256=P (1)	20-6=N (3)		√1=A (2)	
	3+2=E (4)	144/12=L (1)	√196=N (2)	4X5=T (1)	10+4=N (2)	
	√196=N (4)	1+0=A (2)	29-20=I (1)	1X1=A (2)		
		40-20=T (4)				

PAGE 98

		2X8=P (1)		3X4=L (4)	3+2=E (4)	38-19=S (3)
		1-0=A (1)	12+8=T (4)		20-4=P (3)	√625=Y (4)
		2X7=N (4)	18-9=I (1)	√16=D (3)	3X5=O (3)	
		15/3=E (4)	14+4=R (1)	3+2=E (3)	19X1=S (2)	√400=T (3)
	6/3=B (4)	100/5=T (2)	√81=I (1)	25-9=P (2)	10+10=T (3)	
	35/5=G (1)	7+7=N (1)	54/6=I (2)	27/3=I (2)		
			√324=R (2)			

	30-11=S (3)					5+2=G (4)
		12-4=H (3)		16-8=H (2)	2X7=N (4)	
		12/12=A (3)	5X1=E (2)	72/8=I (4)		60/3=T (4)
	32/8=D (1)	√324=R (3)	1+0=A (2)		2X10=T (4)	5X1=E (4)
	12-7=E (1)	256/16=P (3)	√144=L (2)	4+4=H (1)	√529=W (1)	√576=X (4)
	33-28=E (3)	30-16=N (1)	3X3=I (1)	45/9=E (2)		
		42/3=N (3)			2X2=D (2)	

			5+3=H (4)			
		30-12=R (1)	√25=E (4)	3X1=C (4)		
	35-30=E (3)	30-11=S (4)	3X5=O (1)		√196=N (4)	16/8=B (4)
		√169=M (3)	36-18=R (1)	25-7=R (3)	√441=U (2)	55/11=E (4)
		324/18=R (1)	1+1=B (3)	19X1=S (2)	12/12=A (3)	
		√81=I (1)	2X9=R (2)	3+2=E (2)		24/8=C (3)
		76/4=S (2)	11+2=M (1)		50/10=E (3)	

PAGE 101

		35/7=E (3)	√25=E (1)		46-23=W (3)	
	2X9=R (3)	2X4=H (1)	30-8=V (3)	2+2=D (1)	16-8=H (3)	√361=S (4)
		14-11=C (1)	3+2=E (3)		1X1=A (3)	√400=T (4)
	1+0=A (1)			10+10=T (3)	48/3=P (2)	196/14=N (4)
	400/20=T (2)	100/20=E (1)		5X1=E (2)	18-9=I (4)	
	2X7=N (2)	84/7=L (1)	2+1=C (2)	3X6=R (2)	30-12=R (4)	√256=P (4)
		√25=E (2)	10/5=B (1)			

PAGE 102

		√64=H (1)	√289=Q (3)		60/4=O (3)	
		18-9=I (3)	15/5=C (1)	441/21=U (3)	14+4=R (3)	
	√144=L (3)		5X1=E (1)			72/8=I (2)
	2X9=R (4)	3+2=E (1)	2X10=T (2)		2X2=D (2)	
	45/9=E (4)	256/16=P (1)	169/13=M (4)	√225=O (2)	99/11=I (2)	
		10+3=M (4)	35-16=S (1)	42-21=U (4)	90/5=R (4)	24/6=D (4)

			3+2=E (4)			
	18/6=C (2)	16/2=H (4)	2+2=D (1)	√324=R (4)		
	19X1=S (4)	2X9=R (2)	5X1=E (1)			12+7=S (3)
	√1=A (4)	√625=Y (2)		42/6=G (1)	2X4=H (3)	
	46-23=W (4)	2X1=B (1)	30-11=S (2)	√196=N (1)	3X3=I (3)	
		2X10=T (2)	1-0=A (1)	7+7=N (3)		32/8=D (3)
			1+0=A (2)	6+6=L (2)	√25=E (3)	

	20/4=E (4)	√324=R (4)	90/5=R (1)			
	1X1=A (4)	3+2=E (1)	10+8=R (4)	18-9=I (4)	21/7=C (3)	
		121/11=K (1)		1-0=A (3)	√196=N (4)	
		1X1=A (1)	28-14=N (3)	42/3=N (3)	√49=G (2)	49/7=G (4)
	100/20=E (2)	15+4=S (2)	√64=H (1)	108/9=L (2)	25/5=E (3)	
		√361=S (2)	1X1=A (2)	38-19=S (1)	√16=D (3)	
			19X1=S (2)			

PAGE 105

		$10+9=S$ (1)	$10/2=E$ (1)			
	$10-5=E$ (1)		$5X1=E$ (1)			$12-11=A$ (3)
	$30/6=E$ (2)	$24-12=L$ (2)		$56/7=H$ (1)	$26-13=M$ (3)	
	$2X9=R$ (4)	$\sqrt{25}=E$ (4)	$2X2=D$ (2)	$24/8=C$ (1)	$\sqrt{225}=O$ (3)	
$\sqrt{81}=I$ (4)	$72/9=H$ (2)	$5X1=E$ (4)	$\sqrt{196}=N$ (2)			$42/3=N$ (3)
	$38-19=S$ (4)	$\sqrt{1}=A$ (2)	$44/11=D$ (4)		$77/11=G$ (3)	

PAGE 106

			$\sqrt{361}=S$ (3)			
		$48/3=P$ (3)	$33/3=K$ (4)	$10+10=T$ (3)		
		$\sqrt{324}=R$ (4)	$90/5=R$ (3)	$19X1=S$ (4)	$\sqrt{196}=N$ (3)	
	$63/9=G$ (1)	$1X1=A$ (4)	$5X1=E$ (3)	$15/3=E$ (3)	$36-18=R$ (2)	$12+6=R$ (2)
	$2X8=P$ (4)	$10+8=R$ (1)	$14+5=S$ (3)		$22-17=E$ (2)	$4+1=E$ (2)
	$\sqrt{361}=S$ (4)	$25/25=A$ (1)	$57/3=S$ (1)	$3X3=I$ (2)		$\sqrt{25}=E$ (2)
	$12/4=C$ (1)	$3+2=E$ (1)		$28-14=N$ (2)	$24/6=D$ (2)	

PAGE 107

					√400=T (4)	
				33-22=K (1)	1X1=A (4)	
		√256=P (3)	7+5=L (1)	26-13=M (4)	√361=S (1)	
	1+1=B (2)	2X9=R (3)	1X1=A (1)	10+8=R (4)		30-24=F (4)
		60/4=O (2)	1+0=A (3)	16/2=H (1)	3X5=O (4)	
	30-12=R (3)	12/12=A (2)	625/25=Y (3)	2+1=C (1)	76/4=S (2)	
		5X1=E (3)	324/18=R (2)	2X2=D (2)		

PAGE 108

			√16=D (3)			
				√225=O (3)	21/7=C (1)	
	2X9=R (2)			3X3=I (3)	4+4=H (1)	
	1+1=B (4)	100/20=E (2)	2X8=P (4)	√1=A (1)	2X7=N (3)	
	√144=L (4)	30/5=F (2)	√324=R (4)	8+7=O (1)	4+3=G (3)	
	17-12=E (2)	42-21=U (4)		30-11=S (1)		
		10+8=R (2)	38-19=S (2)			

PAGE 109

	13+5=R (1)		43-29=N (2)			
	25/5=E (1)	14-7=G (2)		72/8=I (2)	196/14=N (3)	
	45/9=E (4)	√121=K (1)		√529=W (2)		√25=E (3)
7+7=N (4)	2X9=R (4)	1+0=A (1)	3+2=E (2)	28-14=N (1)	15+5=T (3)	
2+1=C (4)	12+11=W (4)	24/3=H (2)	5X1=E (1)	10+10=T (3)	√361=S (1)	
72/9=H (4)		√9=C (2)	√81=I (3)	2X1=B (3)		

PAGE 110

	√324=R (2)	3+2=E (2)	30-16=N (3)			
	√256=P (2)	25/5=E (1)	√49=G (3)	18-9=I (3)		
	2X2=D (1)	13+3=P (2)	5+6=K (1)		√16=D (3)	
	225/15=O (2)	48/3=P (4)	2X8=P (4)	√1=A (1)	10+4=N (3)	
	13/13=A (4)	√64=H (2)	2+3=E (4)	3X5=O (1)	15-14=A (3)	
10+8=R (4)		19X1=S (2)	16-12=D (4)	36-18=R (3)	25-6=S (1)	
	30-7=W (4)			19-17=B (3)		

PAGE 111

		45/9=E (3)	√361=S (4)	√400=T (4)		
27/3=I (3)	60/5=L (2)	19X1=S (3)	30-14=P (1)	1-0=A (4)	25-6=S (2)
2X2=D (3)		1X1=A (2)	√441=U (1)	3+2=E (2)	5X1=E (4)
225/15=O (3)		676/26=Z (1)	√121=K (2)		16-8=H (4)
	24/12=B (3)	13X2=Z (1)			√529=W (4)
		√25=E (1)	24-12=L (1)		

PAGE 112

		10/5=B (4)			20/5=D (2)	
		3+2=E (4)	√81=I (1)	√25=E (2)		
√144=L (4)	44-22=V (1)	11+3=N (2)	196/14=N (1)	√25=E (3)	
3X5=O (4)	4+5=I (1)	2X9=R (2)	24-21=C (3)	42/6=G (1)	
30-7=W (4)		√324=R (1)	42-21=U (2)	1+0=A (3)	
28-14=N (3)		2X2=D (1)	3X4=L (3)	√400=T (2)	
	5X1=E (3)	√9=C (3)	121/11=K (3)		

PAGE 113

		15/3=E (1)	22-18=D (1)	√225=O (2)		27-20=G (3)	
		√324=R (1)	5X1=E (2)	42/3=N (1)	38-19=S (2)	2X7=N (3)	
	2+1=C (3)		20-16=D (2)	4+5=I (1)	3X3=I (3)		
		√1=A (3)	18-9=I (2)	√400=T (3)	24/12=B (1)		
	32/8=D (4)	2X11=V (2)	361/19=S (3)		12/12=A (4)	15/5=C (4)	
		5X1=E (4)	√169=M (4)	108/9=L (4)			

PAGE 114

			32-16=P (3)				
		3X4=L (3)	19X1=S (4)	√256=P (3)	14-13=A (1)		
		3+2=E (3)	50/10=E (4)	56/4=N (1)	27/3=I (3)		
	1X1=A (2)		√25=E (4)	√49=G (1)		√324=R (3)	
√361=S (2)	30-16=N (2)		5X1=E (1)	2X9=R (4)			
	3+2=E (2)	4+3=G (2)	9+9=R (1)		√400=T (4)		
	144/12=L (2)						

PAGE 115

		2X10=T (1)		√256=P (3)	3X5=O (3)	
	3+2=E (1)		√441=U (1)	7+7=N (2)	2X10=T (3)	
	36/2=R (1)	46-23=W (2)	4+5=I (2)	32-16=P (1)	35/5=G (2)	121/11=K (3)
		√225=O (2)		8+5=M (1)	√361=S (3)	
	√144=L (4)	28-14=N (2)	15/5=C (4)	225/15=O (1)	13-8=E (3)	
	√121=K (2)	20-15=E (4)	√9=C (1)	√576=X (4)		8/2=D (3)
				100/20=E (4)		

PAGE 116

		5+2=G (4)	30-11=S (4)	√529=W (3)		
	196/14=N (4)	√144=L (1)	8+7=O (3)			
	14/14=A (1)	72/8=I (4)	30-12=R (3)		5+3=H (2)	48/3=P (3)
	√400=T (4)	42-21=U (1)		38-19=S (3)	√225=O (2)	3X3=I (3)
	1X1=A (4)	6X4=X (1)		324/18=R (2)	16/2=H (3)	
		√324=R (4)	5X1=E (1)	45/3=O (2)	6+7=M (2)	
		3+2=E (2)	11+3=N (2)	10+9=S (1)		